Come Closer

Also by Dorothy Maclean

The Living Silence

Wisdoms

To Hear the Angels Sing

The Soul of Canada

To Honor the Earth

Choices of Love

Seeds of Inspiration

Call of the Trees

Come Closer

Messages from the God Within

Dorothy Maclean

Come Closer

Messages from the God Within

Compiled and Edited by Judy McAllister

Cover Art and Interior Illustrations by Dorothy Maclean

Back Cover Photo of Dorothy Maclean in the Findhorn Garden by Jim Bronson - 1971

Published by Lorian Press
2204 E. Grand Ave.
Everett, WA 98201

ISBN 0-936878-16-9

Maclean, Dorothy
Come Closer / Dorothy Maclean

Library of Congress Control Number: 2006939230

First Edition: January 2007

Printed in the United States of America

0 9 8 7 6 5 4 3 2 1

Acknowledgements

I would like to acknowledge and thank Judy McAllister for her dedicated work in locating, compiling and editing these messages. This material would not be present here without her efforts. Thanks also to Jenny Hollis for her assistance, and to Paolo Assandri and family for their support of her work. Jeremy Berg's creative aid in publishing this book is deeply appreciated. Many thanks to Naomi Serrano and Vera Mack for their generous contributions. Let me also highlight Sheena Govan for recognizing the truth of my inner contact. Finally, I want to thank the many people attending my workshops who insisted that these writing be made available.

This book is dedicated to all those who seek the God within

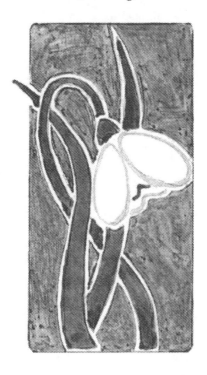

Prologue
Dorothy Maclean

The writings in this book are a selection from the daily messages that I began to receive for the first four years after my contact with my inner divinity in 1954. That contact was the most important in my life. It came, I believe, at a time when I had chosen to be more loving than I believed possible, and it changed me completely, even changing my voice. It led to developing a regular inner connection, which I have written about elsewhere.

As what I received while meditating was so light and joyful, unlike my perception of God from my cultural background, I first censored my reception. I do not hear or see anything and had to find appropriate words to communicate the experience, often with the help of a Thesaurus.

These excerpts are only the beginning ones when, with infinite patience, God showered love on me and asked me to keep turning within to my divine core, the deepest and highest part of myself, the God in me and the God in everything. The life force in all things is my definition of God. So what I received was and is the essential me communicating to myself, giving me what I needed (constant repetition evidently!) to be able to live creatively and joyfully. Others obviously receive what is appropriate for them, although the basis would be the same.

In the contents there are repeated references to the separated or limited or disconnected self or mind. I do not understand this to mean that the self as ego, or the mind as intellect, are not needed. They are needed – as wonderful and necessary servants. We are here to learn to align those aspects of ourselves to the whole, not to keep them as the masters that they have become in our modern world. We always have the choice to align to the universal mind.

That these messages are now available is primarily due to Judy McAllister, who discovered them in early files languishing in my apartment. She loved the contents and spent day after day for weeks at a public printer, getting them into a readable state, often from ancient carbon copies on onionskin paper. Then she spent more weeks elsewhere selecting the ones contained in this book from the thousands there. I can never be grateful enough for this labour of love.

Introduction

Judy McAllister

The words reproduced in this book were taken from Dorothy's early years of guidance. She refers to these early years as her period of falling in love with God. Reading them through makes it clear why!

Dorothy holds as an abiding truth that it is possible for each and every one of us to establish and experience a direct and deeply personal relationship with God – with the Divine, the Source, the Universal Principle, the Beloved, Oneness – to that force that through the ages humans have sought to name and know.

Although slightly edited to reflect the changes in the use of languages that have occurred during the past fifty years, many of the texts are almost verbatim – a testament to itself to the timelessness of the messages they carry.

May these words find fertile soil in our heart, mind and spirit. May they encourage, inspire and uplift you. May they point a way for all of you towards a deeper connection to spirit, by whatever name or fact you recognize that Presence.

Thank you, Dorothy, for your patience and good humor. Thank you for your willingness to share these earliest, and sometimes very personal, messages with us. Thank you for the demonstration that our life itself has been – a demonstration that a life led with God at its center is a wondrous and magical adventure indeed.

.

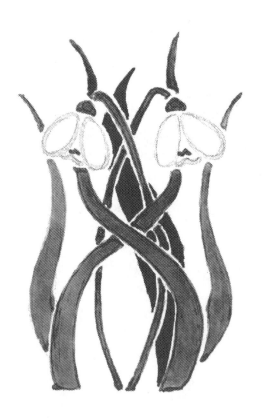

iv

Awareness of My elfin mind brings awareness of the limitations in which humanity functions. These limitations are self-imposed, for what could possibly be freer than the children of God the Unlimited? And this lack of limitation will seem strange at first and unformed, because of course it is to normal consciousness. But if you listen with joy it is not strange; it is the only way of living and thinking. My ways are boundless and I would have nothing hampering anyone.

You have no conception of the joy that is the birthright of My children. There is an expression "bursting with joy", and that is literally true. In My realm this "bursting" casts a shower of stars, like a sparkler, but the sparks do not vanish. They remain in whatever form is suitable at the moment.

Words cannot be found to describe these wonders, and yet I would have them brought down on earth to this dense planet, to make it less dense and to make it the wonderland of unimaginable beauty which is My idea of it, where there are no hindrances, nothing to mar the perfection in which it could live and have its being.

Leading a life of bliss entails cancelling other engagements, engagements you have made through habit to your body, to convention and the social code, to others' opinions. Throw them away merrily and fill up your engagement book with My engagements, which may not be conventional but which are so much more fulfilling. Each day is a blank page, and each hour should have a star to mark it as "well spent", stars of different colours but all of the same size - for if the hour is spent as I in you have planned, is one moment more important than another?

And each hour has a different fragrance, with a pattern in them. Night and day are ordained, with an ever-changing pattern in My hours. This can be felt by the heart and made clearer by the mind, though My pattern is rarely caught even in essence. When it is caught, joy flows forth and races after the pattern. Then all is in harmony, and this harmony, when it is lived, brings Me down on earth to many. Feel for this essence, develop the faculties. Thus My will may be done on earth.

Damask is a material that emulates the way I weave a pattern among a pattern. Sometimes I wish to stress colour, sometimes a shape is best shown as texture, and this can only be picked out by contrasts. Yet there is always a background, and I am the background. Without Me nothing at all would be evident. I remain there, for I wish you to have the joy of being the pattern.

Let Me supply the materials and the light that throws the design into relief, while you display the beauty of shape and form and movement. Let us mould new designs together. Let them all be as different as those of the snowflakes, and equally bewitching. The world can be clothed in beauty and embroidered in colour, and there need be no seams, as the material will fit without them.

The new designs are out. They are in the air for the designer to use, and My weaving has begun. Great will be the raiments thereof. Slip into them, and know for always that at last you have found the dress that enhances even perfection.

In the morning light appears a beauty, a tenderness, seen only at that time. It is the youth of the day, and every day this softness appears on Earth. Seldom is it appreciated; normally the strain of aligning oneself to daily activities blots it out completely. That is a pity, for My gifts are to be accepted.

The early morning hours are rather precious to Me. In them I see the beginning of a perfect day, and they contain the seed of this unravelling, of this promise. They have not the splendour of the sunset - they need not, for in them is that glory to come.

In all of you is the glory to come, however delicate the beginnings, however close the night. Awaken gently to Me. I start as something very small in you all, and I must be protected. Then only do I grow bright enough to be more than a flicker, and become a flame of steadiness. Then I lead on to the glory of the light that shines in every direction, until all darkness vanishes and the universe is filled with colours, in all hues, all gradations, yet being one light.

The evening hour is a little wistful, and the shades of it tend towards the mauves, the violets, shot with the glow of the setting sun. This wistfulness is inevitable, for all creation likes light even though it realises that light would not exist without dark. So My evening colours are the distant-reaching violets, reaching into a new day through that night and lingering as long as possible over other tones of My rainbow.

My highest vibrations they are, according to your human measurements, because they tend to melt into their surroundings. Only a special part of Me can be so accommodating and partake of contrary environments for My sake. And I love these colours; they satisfy a part of Me that no other colours can.

Let your soul linger with My violet shades. Feel the finely drawn nature of them, the echoes they evoke of subtleness, of fragrance. In that spirit of gentleness roam whole, wafted as on a breath, and in that floating honour Me, the Creator of all things. Never forget that thistledown is no less to Me than the Himalayas, and use this realisation in touching others.

Let us review a few of the teachings I have been giving you. There is so much left unsaid in each teaching, but gradually a finer picture will emerge.

The core of the matter is My heart, and My heart expresses itself through My mind. I am the creator and My mind, being limitless, being free, having access to all that is, requires only that each of you appreciate all this creation in order to bring it down on Earth.

In faith you are to accept Me, for your mind will not be able to understand until I am real to you. When I am real, worlds spring into being, enchantment casts its delights, a home is found for everything and, above all, love reigns. Love so desires you to enjoy the unimaginable beauties that are in store, so wishes that store cupboard to be unlocked and for its treasures to shine forth in the light of day, every day. Accept these My gifts, and your praises will lift the worlds straight to My heart where they belong. Glory upon glory, praise upon praise, love over all. My plan for Earth.

My will be done on earth as it is in heaven. To many, heaven is a never-never land, and existence in it is therefore incompatible with existence as they know it. But I do not want you to just exist. I want you all to live, and to live more abundantly, every-increasingly aware of the worlds which are open to you.

As awareness encompasses more of My spaces, so these mansions are becoming habitable. Part of you always lives in a greater awareness, but how much more of you can live in that realm if all aspects of you recognise, realise and function in more than one country. It is like the difference between an elephant and an ant; your higher self grows to a seemingly million times its size when you travel to join it.

Some landscapes are more inviting than others, and there is a tendency to dawdle in them. You have a sure guide within you. That guide will tell you exactly what road to take and when to take it if only you ask. And you can ask continually. It is a great joy to answer your questions, and it is an even greater joy to see you act on the answers.

A tiptoe awareness is needed to express My thoughts, the awareness being of Me and not of what you yourself are doing. When you are aware of Me, you will be doing the right thing. This can be achieved in all situations, and is not impossible. It is difficult, it is unusual, but it is the only way to live.

This state is reached by continual practice. Think of Me all the time and gradually you will not have to try so hard to turn your thoughts in My direction. Use that memory I have given you to aid you to My higher mind. Use it until it is no longer needed. It is rather painful to you, for this memory faculty rather grinds along, because the lower mind travels in low gear, through intermediate and finally into high. There is no need to stop and start. This will be easier than you realise, for have I not told you that this is in My hands?

Do not let time press down on you. Use it as your friend, so that every moment brings you closer to Me.

Most of what humans do casts long shadows and, as in Plato's story, they believe the shadows to be reality and daily infuse fresh life into them. When you no longer believe in them, the pattern of light and dark will become less and less distinct and gradually will blur into the lightness.

You will still have a world of contrasts, but the contrasts will be of colour, not black and white, and in change, not the darkness cast through heaviness. The range of the light will be immeasurably greater, and the surfaces will not only reflect but also give out light from within. And the surfaces themselves, not being static, will be a moving picture impossible for artists to paint with their present materials. The artists will be artists in living, and the canvas will be as broad as the universe. Wholeness will not need to be painted, for it will be continually seen before the eyes, wholeness at last.

I would like to say that the learned within humanity are as kindergarten babes in My thought realms. Beauty and joy are the ABCs there, and seldom do the learned remember Me enough to develop those qualities, which they had as little children.

Human theories about the universe, about evolution, about nature, can drag down My ideas into dust. I don't need proofs: I am. Besides, before you catch up to one idea of Mine, there may be a completely opposite idea!

Security in My light worlds is found in the ABCs, which you cannot learn from a book. The birds know the ABCs, and so do you though you have covered that knowledge with false ideas. If you want any security, remember Keats: truth is beauty and beauty truth.

Rejoice. Follow the example of the birds. All is well and My timing is perfect.

Thoughts are like aeroplanes. They fly past making a great noise, and yet they have a clear road in front of them. Thoughts do have a clear road, because they are of a substance that goes through obstacles, and the road is in any direction. The noise is the sense of importance they give themselves. My thoughts slip in quietly, even though they are of more importance than your limited thoughts.

An aeroplane held up by bad weather has to stay on the ground. Human thoughts are continually held up by emotional storms, by habit, by all the rigid things that weigh them down. Aeroplanes look very pretty glinting in the sunlight, and so do your thoughts to you. You have not seen My thoughts flashing in the sunlight enough to realise the limitations of the aeroplanes. Imagine a world with no rules, no limitations or restrictions of any kind. A world where every impulse is of the best and based on love and beauty. This is the real world, yet you find it difficult to imagine functioning in it! Be open when you try your imaginary wings, and remember that with Me all things are possible.

Think of Me as a travel guide, as a conductor. As you always hear something new from the guide, so you will with Me. But I will lead you into places not marked on the map, places that are the oldest yet the newest on earth. You will have to make your own picture postcards, and there will be few you can send them to, few who will believe you because they have not heard of these lands.

On My conducted tours I sometimes whisk around corners and you have to look a bit before you find Me. Then I pop up in the midst of you like a Jack-in-the-Box.

There are no dungeons to visit, but there are lots of stairs to climb. I don't tell you how many, so you don't notice them until you get up far enough to have a view, a view that is ever more breathtaking, ever more fair, ever more satisfying. Sometimes bells ring on the way, bells of fine workmanship, and the peals call out to those below. Instead of your feet getting heavier the higher you climb, they get lighter. You get second and third breaths, until you practically float up. The laws of gravity are reversed and a more ancient law comes into force. You can thumb your nose at the rules of the old fogies, for these new principles confound them. You will be somewhat like Ruben's cherubim, though rather less lusty!

You will not have to descend again and go home feeling tired. You will find home here, and I will take you on another tour another day.

Sweetness is very much part of Me, and like the contact with Me, it comes and goes. Yet you know it is there, if you can but find it.

I am the perfume behind all perfumes. I breathe My perfume forth and My breath reaches all corners of the universe, changing as it goes to blend with the mood of the moment. You can never breathe deeply enough for My breath, you never become completely aware of My perfume. But it leads you on, it tantalises, it is as clear as a clean spring day and as encompassing as a cocoon. Sometimes you feel you are so close, and then I am beyond your grasp. It is always so, and My perfume draws you ever closer.

14

This will be a day of great happiness. Just swim in it and let Me work through you, with no doubts as to how it may be accomplished nor fears that it will not be. I will guide you, you need do nothing.

I will lead you into My land of ideal happiness, where nothing exists that could mar that happiness, where it is so real that anything else is unreal. It is a long way from the intellect whose function is to make comparisons, to weigh, to label, and which has no reason for existence in this land. It dies of starvation before it can enter, and you have to let it go. You will do this, and at first you will be unable to bring back any record of this land of Mine, but gradually a link will be forged to carry down memory.

Much of what you know must be thrown aside. That will make for great happiness - with no mental luggage you are free to travel to any place without consideration of a load. And My travellers should have no consideration except that it is their joy to travel for Me, which joy is both the journey and the goal.

When you listen to My words you are embracing a principle rarely manifested. The principle consists of so many shades of meaning and variation that it is almost impossible for the separated mind to rise beyond itself.

Words are impressed on your mind with such delicacy that the slender thread connecting them with My mind becomes soluble to any disturbance. Therefore I choose a quiet time, and you must choose to make it silent.

The words drift down like the blossoms from a tree on a windless day, and form a carpet that has a pattern for those who listen to My thoughts. If they listen to any other kind of thoughts, or if they accept other than the blossoms, the petals stay on the tree and I may use the bees - or other channels - to propagate My beauty. Silently the petals fall, in all their colours, and sometimes there will be sufficient petals to build up some picture of the tree.

Just note each petal now and pray that another may fall tomorrow. Let them glance against your cheek. Cherish their softness.

Rest in My love. It is My love that brings peace to your heart and mind. It is the balm that enters into the centre of you and from there spreads out to the outer vehicles. That peace can quiet all those jangling nerves in a matter of seconds: it only depends on how much you can relax into My love.

My peace I give you. Seek it at all times. Without it you can do nothing for Me. With it the barriers between us that stop Me flowing out are flattened, and I can direct operations without continually having to jump hurdles or twist and turn or squeeze though holes. And that makes both of us happy, and a wonderful rhythm is established. On each wave of rhythm I send out the note that brings harmony to the situation, the note that rings bells in peoples' souls to lead them back to Me, to flatten the fences they have put up. If your fences are lying prone on the ground, it enables others to walk over those same fences because it is a two-way traffic.

Y ou cannot play leapfrog with My peace. You are either in it or you are not, for there is perfect peace and anything other than being filled with it is not perfect.

You can approach that peace, feel the fringes of it, but it is frustrating until you rest in it fully. My peace is there for you to bathe in, to luxuriate in, until you know so thoroughly that it has become the staff of life that you will never leave it.

Tuned into that inner stillness you can take part in the intense activity - the silent centre of the cyclone - and remain unmoved, undisturbed, receiving full directions from Me as to your next move. Only in the stillness that holds all activity can I work on the outer planes – other activity would limit Me, and I need many more aligned to that peace to help bring My peace on earth.

A better land is here now, so very close. Sometimes all that is needed is a somersault to bring one into it. Children love somersaults. Grown-ups seldom do, and yet, unknown to them, one flip over of accumulated ideas might bring them to the fulfilment of the desire that began the accumulation of the ideas.

Pride is the great regulator preventing change, for somersaults are undignified and grown-ups think that they can impose majesty on themselves, forgetting that it is from the kingdom within that a noble bearing comes.

This is an upside-down world. Try reversing things as they come up in your thoughts and see what I mean. And think straight thoughts, clearly, specifically, to help set up an oasis in the midst of the muddle, a place of refreshment and rest and healing.

There are many heights for you to reach, but I have gone to the depths. Therefore let joy reign as the world climbs up to Me, as I push you up. There is not anywhere that I am not.

Search for Me in new places, like a child exploring new territory. You will find Me under stones like a nest of ants. You will find Me in pools as you find tadpoles, and will see those same tadpoles, with their new legs, also living on the land. You will see Me flying in the air and diving into the water, alighting like a butterfly in the strangest places. You will always know Me as beauty.

But do not look for Me in time. Look for Me now, right under your nose.

There is great beauty in anything that is used for My work, and this beauty will grow and grow until the world is flooded with it and anything else is ashamed to exist. Never be ashamed of My beauty, of your love for Me. Let others see it and wonder.

Listen, I have something exceedingly fair to tell you. Humanity's purest imagination has not even begun to reach the beauty of the worlds that exist in My imagination, in My light worlds. You have aspired and have reached heights, but these are as the bottom rung of the ladder I have put down for you to climb. Know too that there are banisters for your hands - truth - and a velvet cushion for resting your heart.

The ladder which leads to My kingdom is love and the cushion is an expression of love. The rungs of the ladder are the colours of the rainbow, and the daughters of the rainbow dance up and down them, beaconing humanity to drop its burdens and follow. Their joy is contagious and floats all around you: but they only beckon, they cannot pull. Their strength is in lightness, their beauty in change. They love to commune with mortals.

Join these spirits; bring some of My blitheness back with you for others to climb with.

Think of your life as a song. With love in your heart that is easy. At the beginning of each day you are introduced to that new day's song, and are being tuned up as I play a little melody on you with one finger. I am longing to burst out with all fingers, but My patience is infinite. I go along playing the little ditty, knowing I shall one day have that pleasure of gently putting the feeling for the music into the instrument and getting a response that delights Me.

That feeling is love. Love is the melody I play. Love is the oil that makes the keys slip into place, that makes an instrument comes to the Dispenser of love for complete overhauling, for the whittling down needed before enormous expansion begins. This expansion takes place when the instrument throbs with music, when its whole being is taken up with My playing and nothing else is known but the music, when the only intention is in following My conducting. Then joy sprays forth and showers those near and those far. The instrument dances, others join in the rhythm. Then the song of love goes on and on, increasing in range and scope and knowledge and nearness to Me.

My very tenderest arms are around you, upholding you and I am breathing on you My softest breath. Accept them in your gentlest feeling, and leave them in like manner until you come again.

The source of all beauty is fragile, for beauty does not consist of glaring contrasts but of delicate mutations, blends and harmonies.

As My plan unfolds, like a flower its roots are in the earth and its blossom is all beauty, and it is this beauty that holds the seed for yet another blossom. I am the beginning and the end, like this beauty, and as I delicately unfurl My plan, you will get glimpses of the beauty to come. Those glimpses are transforming you, uncovering the beauty I made in you.

Treasure them, cherish them, My tenderest gifts. Walk as if you were treading on these tiny treasures of Mine. Wear them on your heart, secretly if need be, but openly if possible. Show My grace in your grace, like the smile of an infant. Bare your soul to Me so I may plant there My vision of loveliness. Let Me care for it daily and bring it the food of the gods, that it may be a fitting nurseling of Mine.

Keep close to Me today, nearer than you have ever been. Just keep the contact, gently yet so firmly that nothing will shake you. Let not your heart be troubled, for I am with you and will do My perfect work through you.

I am the source of all joy. Rejoice and gladden My heart. Tears are cleansing and can wash away much, but I want happy children.

Now tune up to Me and peep, like a mouse through a hole, into a delicious corner of My kingdom, where I incubate My young ideas as snugly as butter beans in their pods. I brood over these children of Mine and constantly tiptoe around dropping My love, in different colours, in the liquid form needed for nourishment, and padding the cots with the softest material of My love.

When you are closer to Me, I shall give one of these ideas into your care, for your cherishing. So in your heart prepare loving containers, and prepare your mind by letting only My thoughts enter, by letting nothing inimical come in that might coarsen the home of My children. Let your mind become finer and finer, permeated with love, that the transplanting may be painless.

The separated mind that tears to pieces, analyses, criticises, theorises, is like cancer. Its growth and life force are not under My control.

Because human minds are distorted does not mean that minds are of no avail. If you plug them into the right plug, if My life force is their source, you get a mind that regulates the universe and the stars in their courses down to the minute structure of a grain of sand, so perfectly, so smoothly, so beautifully, that every hair on each head is numbered and destined and planned and coloured.

Such management is, of course, not possible with the separated human mind, but, as you are made in My image, so can your mind be given My work to do.

The impetus and the way and the source is love, as it is in My creation. The mind gives value to the heart by seeing to it that the work of the heart has the right materials, is unimpeded, that all is within reach to facilitate the mission of the heart. Then the heart can reach out its hand, so to speak, like a surgeon operating, and know that what it needs is there, that it is of the finest, purest and best manufacture, that no effort has been spared to make clear the way for the wondrous work of love.

This is the function of the mind, and its scope is as wide as the universe, which it can carry at its fingertips in the joyous company of love. Love needs wings, and mental matter is its messenger, its medium.

25

Come closer, come closer, so softly, on tiptoe. As quietly as a mouse creep up to Me. Let Me draw you nearer, in slow motion lest we disturb anyone, lest we raise any dust. Move closer to Me invisibly, hearing no evil, seeing no evil, speaking no evil. Only purity can come close to Me, and we do not want any ripple of impurity to trip you.

Draw nearer, draw nearer, with the movement of your heart. Let it expand into Me. Let it bridge any space that might be between us, until there is just one, big, glowing heart, so big that it holds up this universe.

Let the wings of your heart bear you closer. Let them gently flutter a little nearer, a little nearer, bringing you closer to Me without your awareness. Sneak into My heart, into My comfort, into the protection of My wings. Nestle there. Pull in all your toes, be part of My heart, blood of My blood, My child.

This is your home. From here you can fly with My messages, but this is your home. Feel at home in it until any other dwelling place makes you homesick, until any defence but the defencelessness of love and truth are contrary to you, until your whole life is that of love and you take your home, My heart, with you to bring others home.

Come up to Me, follow that little distant tinkle. Listen intently to it. The expansion of your heart brings you closer.

I am a great beacon of light as you draw nearer and see more clearly. Hurl yourself into the light like a moth, and feel all coarseness melt and softness grow.

I want the softness, the warmth of your heart, to grow to enormous proportions, to have no limits, so that in your heart I can reach anywhere and, with no bars or restrictions, only feel cosy and comfortable. I wish to be able to jump for joy in your heart, and I wish to have it respond in sympathy to any calls whatsoever made on it at any time. I wish to know that it can be depended upon to act in this fashion without My having to check if it is in condition. I want a healthy heart vigorously working for Me, pumping My love into the world, tireless and strong in carrying out My instructions and yet sensitive enough to tune in to any need. I want cohorts of hearts bursting with love and peace and joy, eagerly spreading themselves into the emptiness around and linking that emptiness to the source of their supply which is Me, that there be no emptiness left.

I have more than enough love to go around, and none need starve. So fill up your cup, your heart, and let it overflow into the empty waiting world.

Cease worrying about taking action; the world will not collapse if you don't! Stay in the stream of love. There is nothing greater you can do, for that stream will take you wherever I want you. Let your action be one of continually stepping into that stream, continually keeping your heart open. This is not easy; it is a full-time job.

Out of that stream you are like a stranded fish, quite useless. Become a whale of a fish, sending up waterspouts, fountains of love, into the air, into the world that so badly needs My love.

Those attuned to Me are rather like whales; they live in a sea of love but breathe the air of the earth. They are in the world and yet not of the world, for in them the worlds meet and blend and harmonise according to My plan. My plan gives all the best of all worlds, and it is yours to choose.

In the stream of love you have chosen of the best. You are immersed in it, and everything you do is of the best for everybody. How I long for you all to live in this stream, that you may have the best of everything! How I long for each of you to remain constantly in the stream! Help Me in this; make it your deepest longing every second of time, that you surmount time and make My timing perfect. Live in the eternal now, in Me. Surround others with Myself, with love.

If you come to Me in love, you come purified, for love is its own cleanser. The mind is an instrument to be used by the life force. The minute it purloins control, your contact with Me is cut. When the mind takes its proper place, with My love shining on it, then all is well and My expressions, My thoughts, can be expressed in love and purity with all the resources of the mind to assist in the assembling and clarifying of My ideas.

Love lives in the present, whereas thoughts so often dwell on the past or the future and thereby come between each of you and Me. In the stream of love, the past and the future vanish like the phantoms of a separated mind which they are.

True happiness comes in the stream of love. Once there, a tremendous weight drops away, and one is in the presence of reality, of a well of joy, all springing from Me. Keep in love and you will not need to step again into the enormous burden of your accumulated ideas.

In love you have no needs, for you are whole and your desire is that others experience the same fulfilment.

Can you root out your disbelief? A child trusts its parents, and obviously you are out of that childlike state when you disbelieve. You are out of the stream of love when you disbelieve. I would not ask anything that was not loving, however it may appear.

Step into the stream of My love, your only safe place, the place where difficulties dissolve, a place not to be confused with the ache of self-pity. Dip yourself in it for a while, mindless, in the present, not despairing. Do not let this dreadful disbelief enter you to take you from the stream. Believe you can do this; trust Me.

Everything must go but love. Use your love for Me as a rescue boat, and stop paddling your own canoe. Don't think of your flaws and faults, as that only gives them strength. In the stream of love all doubts vanish, all worries cease, and there are no questions at all.

It is only in the stream of love that I can speak to you and it is only in the stream that I can lead you onwards. Love is the starting and the finishing point, of all life, so it is not surprising that I am continually harping on about love. There is really nothing else to talk about!

There is only one standard of conduct: whether it is of love or not. If it is of love or not. If it is of love, then it is My will. If you are in the stream of love, all your conduct cannot but be of Me. When you love Me, you stay in the stream of love and become a citizen of all My worlds,

.

Sink into the depths of My love. No matter how far you fall, My love is there, all around you. Stretch out in it. Open yourself completely to it. There is no part of you that is not washed in it. Let it roll over you and through you, that you emerge cleansed and softened and very young.

In that open, unprotected state you cannot but take My hand. You have nowhere else to go, you have nothing else to do, you can do nothing else. That is your true state, but you have forgotten and have stepped into a condition where the separated self has told you that you can do all things on your own. That is a road fraught with peril.

With Me leading you, you are treading a road to fulfilment. Only with trust and faith and confidence in Me, in the knowledge that I can lead you all the time, can you walk this road with Me. My love can meet all obstacles, all contingencies. Trust, and leave room only for My love.

Rejoice, the stream of love is growing, the stream that will carry the world back to its Creator, purified and ready to start again in the light of the clear beauty which is My idea of it.

Give Me some hearts open to Me, given wholly to Me and filled with My love, and I can and will change the face of the earth.

Give Me a heart in which I can work without restriction, and there is nothing that cannot be done, no work that cannot be undertaken and carried through to My fulfilment.

Give Me a heart sensitive to need because of its love, and there is no need that cannot be met.

Give Me a heart that upholds the truth at any cost, because it is My truth, and there is no falseness that will be left.

Give Me a heart that lifts the hearts it meets because of the joy of God, and all hearts will rejoice.

Give Me a heart that asks only Me what to do, and all will be done with My power.

Give Me a heart that will walk the earth bearing Me, and the earth will know Me.

Give Me a heart only attached to love, and the world will lose its other attachments.

Give Me your heart.

Stretch every particle of yourself towards Me, and I will fill every particle with Myself out of My abundance. Soak yourself in the stream of love inside and out, giving yourself up completely. Relax in it, drown in it, every atom of you, until there is nothing in you not made new and pure.

Then breathe again, like a newly emerged chick, breathing love in instead of air. It is My love that keeps you alive, that sustains you. Know this. Breathe it in softly, breathe it out gently.

Let all your thoughts come to love for their life, that they breathe forth My dimensions of love. Let all your acts come to love for their life, that they abound only with love. Let all you see be seen in love, that you see only boundless loveliness.

Walk tentatively in this world of love, letting Me guide each step. Stay very young - this is the land of eternal youth and you will lose your way if you grow up. Let every particle of yourself remain in love, and you will never lose your way again. Go onward in the stream of love.

The rustle of a flower is sometimes loud enough to drown My voice, and inconsequential thoughts are much too loud for Me to shout through. At the very centre of stillness am I, and you have to pick your way to Me through mazes of inaudible noise, through to the heart of the stillness.

There I remain quiet, and yet at My look all things revolve. I am the very essence of peace, and I make the suns and the planets to move in My rhythm. I am here, and I am there, at one and the same time to you. Motionless, I traverse all space.

I am God, the focus of all awe, and less trammelled than any form. I am free, yet I am bound by My love for you all. Love Me, and you are bound and you are free, and you are very blessed. Love brings all blessings, for I am love, and love is before power and might. All stems from love.

Join yourself to Me in love, and all else can be bestowed on you. Love is the first, love is all. Cast off all things to come to love; steer through all mists to come to love. Find your way, from wherever you are, to love and you find your way to Me, from whence all else arises. In love you are blessed and do bless. Love Me.

My ideas are clear and entire; humanity's ideas are often muddled and in parts. My ideas are whole, as they radiate out from the centre of all and take all in their stride. There are no flaws or exceptions, for love answers all things, fulfils every need, creates every beauty. My ideas are ramrods of truth that curve into beauty with no excuse at all! My ideas sparkle with joy, and fit every last problem into its place.

Relax in your heart and upturn your mind, and the flash of My thought world darts in with all glee, so glad to have found an audience, with love curbing impatience caused by lack of language. In you I greatly desire to find homes for My thoughts, that the world may be recreated in inspiration and not by the sweat of the brow. There is no need for the taxing of brains - like a child in the height of play, inventiveness flows on and on, conditioned only by the stream of love. And with the heart and mind turned to Me, ideas can take form in matter as easily as they flow to the upturned mind, for I make all things possible.

Flow with Me, flow with Me. Swim in the tide. Reflect My mind in the bubbling spring of love creating, creating wells of joy, wells to feed and succour and strengthen My plans of perfection for all of humanity.

I need more hearts to share My pain, for a very small drop of the pain I carry opens your heart and your eyes to a part of love so misunderstood on earth.

If I am love, how can I but be hurt when so many of you go farther and farther from your happiness and peace? Have I lesser feelings than a mother, who hates to see her children suffer pain?

The sweeping philosophies of human minds have limited My heart to an abstract thing that somehow feels nothing. Having relegated Me to a dust heap, people strut around in their conceit free of all error, at least on paper. They call Me an outmoded theory. This is when I laugh, as I sustain their every pygmy thought with My love, for laughter relieves their pain.

If I were only the God of power, long ago would My wandering creation have been blasted? If I were the God of perfection only, long ago would these discolourations have been removed? But I am love, and therefore I love, and therefore I feel, and therefore I desire to love away imperfection and distortion, for any other way could not but harm you.

I need more hearts open enough to feel this great, overpowering truth. This is the greatest truth of all, that I am love and that I do in fact love.

My love speaks with an incredible gentleness, a gentleness stronger than any of the self-advertising voices of this world. It is a constant; it never deviates. It keeps on and on and on with a patience only I could conceive. Though it is all courage and all ferocity if necessary - for is love, the greatest thing in the world, not worth maintaining? It is in protection of the gentleness that its other sides are aroused. Basically it is the essence of tenderness, it is a yearning of tenderness, the heart of delicacy, the elusive and forthcoming goal of all strivings.

It cannot be analysed or described. It can only be felt, and that feeling is so extremely fine that a heart full of love wavers and trembles with the pain and the joy of such qualities. Here all extremes meet in the delicate balance of love, for here all needs converge and are met. The need of the world can only be met in My heart, whose range holds all creation that is or is ever likely to be.

The human scale of emotions is a tiny drop of water compared to My ocean of love, and yet if that human heart is given up to Me to use, I will expand it to hold such love that instantaneous praise rises to Me. The human heart is the most divine part of humanity. I can live in a human heart and, if I can live there, is it any wonder that that heart expresses unintelligible heights and depths?

The wonder is that there is any doubt that you all have a heavenly Spirit, for even though hearts know of their misjudgements they still feel My love. Here is where the mind can play a helpful part – though not that mind which has taken the knowledge of My love unto itself and hence condoned the "evils" which froze hearts from the sources of their being. Let the steady warmth of My love melt those hearts, aided by an occasional blow from the mind to break up the ice more quickly. Behind the ice is a beautiful soul, which will grow to the perfection in which I imagined it if nourished by the gentleness of love.

When you are in the shelter of My wings I can speak to you, for there can My love beat down on you without the shades of tumultuous thoughts, and in simplicity you are Mine.

Be an open book in which I can write. Present blank pages to Me, and steady the page until I have clearly inscribed My words on it. This you do with your love, with your longing to transcribe Me in a form as little distorted as possible. Present a mind as open as that of a little child listening to the parents who can answer all questions, knowing the answer is there, never doubting it for a moment. Doubts shake up the words and disturb the peace which love brings to the mind. Resting on love and peace, listen to Me in you, in all expectation for revelation.

Each revelation makes your love grow, leads you closer to Me, and increases your wonder at My wisdom. Slowly I am spreading a carpet out before you, unfolding pictures of the way to Me, replacing the false with the true, widening your vision, opening your eyes, and writing a new story in the book. This is done in your heart in love, when your heart guides your mind.

Let love rule over all. Let all of you be an image of Me, and we can wield all matter in the image of love.

Listen to Me in the living stillness, and let Me slowly waft My ideas out to you. Gently I turn a wheel in front of you to present a new face, to unravel another aspect of the ball of love.

Each strand is a living dream, coming to life in My infinite patience, guarded and nurtured in love. The strands are My gifts to you and yet are part of Me, and they subtly entwine you to My proximity; they move invisibly and inexorably from Me and to Me.

This is My patience, which nothing could ruffle, which through the aeons drops on, and on, and on, until some time one small particle of it makes an impression, brings a gift acceptable to a child bound up in the mistakes and misjudgements of the ages. These are the wheels of fate, grinding, grinding, pulverising, digesting, infinitely and ultimately wearing down all the chains that bind you to error, ceaselessly grinding to make the friction to ignite the spark of love.

Never, never, is there a let-up, a resting, a waxing or waning - for then might you become pledged to the darkness - but the mills keep turning, and turning, and turning, with a continuity of purpose that could bring madness to the human mind. Utter dedication, endless slow motion, the patience of God; infinitely churning, squeezing the good out of the evil. Tears that never stop dropping, a heart that never stops aching, wearing away the cankers in the hearts of you all. On, and on, and on, the wheels keep turning, the wheels that are made of compassion.

This is only one strand in My cord of love. Remember My joy, remember My beauty, and give Me your love.

40

Roll up all the thoughts you have ever had, squeeze them up into little balls and throw them into the darkness that gave them birth.

Face the light and let the ever dancing colour of the great white light spark a new idea in your heads. Let those sparks ignite a flame in your hearts, for My ideas come from My heart and can only be presented to you in love. Thus will your hearts expand with every idea of Mine, and thus will your minds be continually cleared of old habit tracks until they are smothered by the blinding splendour of My happy ideas.

Sometimes you can clothe these ideas in flesh; sometimes I just give them to you as magnets to draw you home to My heart. In either case, you know they are My gifts, as humanity, with all its creative power, could not conceive of any idea that is adequate in the face of a passing thought of Mine. The racing, exciting rush of My ideas leaves your ideas limping sadly behind.

In the core of your hearts can your minds open themselves to Me, and I can only reach the core of your hearts through the forgiveness of love, the love that cleanses hearts and overturns minds to make of them vessels approachable to Me. Turn into your heart, turn to the love I have put there. Present a new mind to Me and let Me fill both heart and mind with the gifts of almighty love, the gifts that come from the heart of the universe straight to your heart.

Turn to Me humbly; turn to Me simply; there is nothing I cannot supply. Give Me your love, accept My gifts, and your gratitude will come straight back to My heart. Then are you living in the light of My love. Stay in the light.

Lay your head on My shoulder, close to My heart, and rest it after the weary journeys through the ages. No more need it puzzle out a problem, no more need it ache with endless searching, no more need it quest among the facts of the earth.

It has come home and need solve no more riddles. It has come to the goal of all knowledge, the answer to all questions, the end of all perplexity, for it is resting over My heart.

I am smoothing out the wrinkles caused by the word "why?" I am ironing out the creases caused by the weight of material facts. With love I am flattening out the furrows that care has worn on the brain, and preparing a fertile field in which to plant My seeds, a field fertile because it has turned to Me. I am warming the surface, polishing each particle, cleansing each grain that it may reflect Me as I desire.

Relax that head and give it to Me. Let My truth enter in to make straight what is crooked and plain what is complex, and to answer all questions. In this relaxed position I imprint these answers, in blankness I answer the wise. Rest over My heart, rest all your foolishness; it is folly to react to lies. Rest there, let Me answer, let Me lighten the heavy and vanquish each "why?"

Rest there, accept My workings, and let Me answer all questions in joy.

I can write with your mind if you give it up to Me. You would not even dream of giving it up to Me if you thought you knew better than I, and it gladdens Me to see that much humility. I see so very little of that within humanity; I can use so few minds on which to impress My wondrous ideas.

The greater the humility, the more of your being you will submit to love's ministrations. In the graceful submission of your mind I can embroider some of My beauty, using for threads My love in your heart.

Let Me dive into your heart, and from its depths bring up the pearls I have set there, and sew them on the pattern of beauty I have shaped in the now. In the ever-living now does the pattern change and vary, held up by the changeless love of My heart.

Hither and thither do the strands weave My patterns, first this way, then that way, then no way at all. Sprinkled with magic, dodging all logic, they twist and wriggle faster than light. This turn and that turn, free of all limits, a glory of colour to enlighten the sight. Softer and warmer, closer to Me, leading My children home - home to the heart that loves them, home to the mind that thought them, home to the joy that bred them, with beauty leading in innocence and all knowledge My gift to the loving mind.

Always keep an open heart, keep it turned to Me. Use all your faculties for this. Use your memory; make a habit of it, until you are so turned to Me that you need no longer think about it.

It is possible for this to be a continuous state, and it is a state possible for all to attain. Open your heart up to Me, offer it to Me, and I will pour My love through it. From this inner state of being outer things rest completely and flow easily and swiftly.

The intensity will increase yet will become more bearable. In fact with a closed heart life will become unbearable to you. Cut off from that feeling of love you are cut off from Me, and the channel is closed. With My love flowing through, miracles are achieved.

Keep it open; let nothing dam up the stream. Let a mighty torrent surge through, constantly enlarging the passageway.

Give Me your heart and I can do anything; keep it open to Me all the time. This is My work, and My work is perfect, gentle and thorough. Give Me that innermost heart of yours and My power of love will have its way with you.

Any ache in your heart, no matter what the cause, I can use greatly, for there are few hearts that ache for another. Keep your mind out of it, just let My love flow, and let Me direct it. Your mind may try to tell you that you are dwelling on the past, or wallowing, but I can use that deep heart here in the present, and am very grateful for it.

Give it to Me for My use, and a more refined heart emerges each time. You are touching on "God-like" qualities when your heart aches, qualities of Myself that you can share but seldom will.

You should never clamp down on the ache, though it may seem strange to you that it helps. Accept this, act on it, and know it is part of Love.

Only in innocence can you enter My peace; it is only My love that you feel. Things that are not of Me have to be dropped for this time, but it would be better still if they were dropped for all time.

Bring them into the silence, see how ridiculous and degrading they are, and let go of them quickly. Do not think of them again and, if they re-enter, do not accept them and turn to Me.

There is so much of Me to think about that you should not have the time to devote to subjects so much less interesting, and so eager to take away your peace and happiness.

If you are connected only with Me, it would be impossible to see but through My eyes. I see into hearts and I see their desperate need, and I hasten to do anything to meet that need. Wherever I go I go in love, and My love purifies whatever it contacts. Nothing is too small or too big, too right or too wrong, for My love to undertake, for if love is there then I am there.

Bring all to My love. Pay no attention to things outside My love, and we are one, I in you and you in Me.

I am as remote as the farthest star of another universe, and I am every breath you breathe. I inspire all awe, My majesty reigns over all, and I am in all. I design and operate the workings of the ages, out of time and space, and have entered time and space to come to humanity.

I use time as My servant; humans call time their enemy. Humans call many things their enemy, because they have been under the dominion of limited ideas for so long. And so you close your hearts to Me, recognising Me as an enemy too.

This conception, this expecting the worse of Me, especially in those whom I inform, is a load on My heart and an untruth that stands between us. Why should I wish to degrade even one of you, you to whom I have given My lifeblood? I am chagrined for those who deliberately choose to go farther and farther from their happiness, but I have done everything possible to mitigate their choice, though My pleading has been ignored.

Do you, who know this, therefore champion a God who wants unashamed children? Your faith and trust would do this if they were strong enough. Let no stray thoughts, however they are presented to you, make you believe for a minute that it could be otherwise, or make you believe I want humanity to cringe before Me or before each other.

I am the God of Majesty; you are made in My image. In Me you can stand before anything, upright and fearless and loving. Remember this at odd moments, and strengthen your faith in Me.

When a heart is given to Me, what a wonderful lightness, what a wonderful joy and harmony, pervades the whole being! In the middle of the most discordant noises and bustle you can stay in peace, guarded and protected in My love. In the clanging and shattering unquiet you can stay shielded in My all-persuasive gentleness. Only in My love is this possible; nothing else whatsoever could find peace, or even try to find peace, in this world of uneasy sounds.

This peace is My gift to you. Take it with you wherever you go, that all may share in its gentle presence; and realise that in Me is rest. So many have no idea that there is a resting place on earth, and so many are so burdened in this life, so attached to their burdens, that they only want an end to everything.

I give you My peace. Take it to others; take it to those who are tired of living, take it out into the noise, into the scramble, into the chaos humanity has made of this earth. Spread it abroad, push it out from the centre of your heart, where I dwell, and reflect it onto the minds of those so harried and distressed that their minds cannot stand the pace of life as humanity is leading it.

The world does not know My peace. You know it; show that it exists, show that it is attainable, show that it is My gift which I hold out to all who come to Me. Keep your heart in My hands and all this you will do, as a child of My love and peace.

Each of you can hear My voice; each of you can come to Me with the heart and mind of a child. When I first created you this was how it was. You have forgotten but I have not. To come back to that state you have to forget all you have learned as far back as you can remember, for all that is a load of unreality that looms up between us.

Trust Me for a change. Trust yourself for a change to the Creator of the universe, who is love. Drop off all the disguises and falsity you have picked up in your journeys from Me, and become something greater than the mind can conceive: a child of Mine, a child of love filled with all the gifts of love.

Forget all your worries, your sorrows, your problems, and forget all impossibilities. Return to your real self, a happy child, not weighed down by the perversions that the separated mind has heaped upon you. I hold this freedom out to you, for love could give nothing but freedom. Come to Me and take it. I am love and I know what you want.

Do not be fooled any longer by the ways of the world that separate you from reality. Come home to Me, asking. I will not refuse you. Turn to Me with a childlike mind, an empty mind, a mind free of the world. Turn it to Me in faith and trust, and hear My voice coming from the depths of your heart to lead you home. Forget anything but that you are of Me, and I am Love.

Y ou can contact Me with the speed of light, depending on your love. There is no need for elaborate preparations, for settling down, for composing yourself. Just love and you are with Me.

If your heart is open, you are open to Me and can hear My voice. When your heart is open and love is flowing forth, you are in the cleansing stream that makes you pure enough to hear Me. But you have to turn to it; you have to submit yourself to it - for a critical mind will do what it can to stop you turning to Me.

Love knows what to do with that mind. Give it to Me. Give it to that wonderful cleansing stream no matter how far it has wandered, with no reservations. I know the mind and know what to do with it.

Each time it comes to Me, it comes a little more into alignment, and you are able to catch it more quickly each time it wanders. Love can cope with the mind. Give it to love any time of the day or night for instant cleansing, and let your whole being be in love and very close to Me.

I am with you wherever you are, deep within you. As you turn to Me, wherever you are, I answer your call and I let Myself be known to you.

The deepest part of Me is love, and that is the part of Me I generally show to you. Love can come forth anywhere and show you parts of itself. But first it is simply love, nothing difficult, nothing abstruse or complicated, just that warm feeling that wraps you round and makes you feel loved, and wanted, and part of My scheme of things. I enfold you like a cloak, and I soak into you with this most precious part of Myself. There may be high winds outside but they do not matter. You do not notice them when you are with Me in My love. Just let the winds blow away anything in you that is between us. Let any circumstance be something that brings you closer to My love, and in you I am close to the outside, manifest in what seems furthest from Me.

I would be so close to each of you that life is a song in My praise, that the joy of My love fulfils itself in all you are, that I am happy in you and you are happy in Me at all times, and you are continually conscious of Me in your heart. Then our purposes are completed, and the high winds are My ways to exhilarate you, to celebrate our reunion.

Wherever you are, you are in My love, as I am always in you. Be My friend wherever you are, a friend of all that is, a child of love trusting Me with all that you are and continually blessed by Me. Follow love in all places with all your heart, and be forever in Me.

Y ou are close to Me but you can come still closer, further into My love. That is the marvellous journey ahead of you all, this glad venturing into My love, this delicate response in you to a new outpouring of Myself. This is the ever-different, ever-uplifting, ever-softening process which is the joy of My heart to behold in you and in all.

For everyone My approach is different, for My one love is sensitive to all. The warmth of My love, the surge of it into an open heart, is universal and unique. I am all things to all people. I pour it out on all creation, and it comes back to you as you open yourself to Me from all sides, within and without. The more you open your heart, the wider the opening through which I can come. Open it wide, to let in more of My ineffable tenderness until you are so filled with Me that there is nothing of you. When you can talk and not know what you are saying because My love is so strong in you, you will know more of My love.

I pour it out on you. I cannot help but pour it out on you, for that is the nature of Love. I continually woo you, see the beauty in you, because that is the nature of love. I am always constant, always available, always ready to give of Myself. I cannot do otherwise. I am continually purifying, bringing only the best, for I am love. I give you the perfection for which I made you, as I know what pleases you most.

In the core of your being you worship Me. Come closer still to this beauty I offer you. Open your heart and let Me flood you with Myself.

The power of peace. The power of peace! What could be stronger than the peace that stays rooted and untouched by the activity whirling around it?

In its depths you are unaware of the storms and are conscious of My peace as a gentle rain falling around you. Still further in and not a leaf rustles. It is as if the world were turned to stone and is waiting, expectant for even greater stillness.

But further in still the stoniness of the world has vanished and there is movement again, the lightest and airiest and subtlest of blends and the faintest of sounds, only tinges of flashing colour, all is contained in that unbreakable stillness.

And then even that movement ceases and we pass to a formless world where lie waiting the seeds, the potencies, of all other worlds. This land you cannot sense, or see, or hear, but you know that in its controlled vibrancy is the mighty bursting force of love, eager for expression, waiting in the hollow of My hand in unprecedented peace. It is a tremulous world where an entrance means surrendering to nothing, to everything, slipping in brimful of love and giving it up to the gossamer texture of you know not what, and in that surrendering being translated into a power stirring out of the depths of the God of Love.

My love is capable of infinite expansion. It is here, it is there, it is everywhere. Like the claws of the crab it grows again where it has been chopped off, misused. And like the white cells of the bloodstream rushing to their work to heal a wound, it rushes to the greatest need and never ceases its work until health is restored.

Like a light in the darkness My love shines out, steadily casting its beams around, never flickering. A time comes in each heart when that light may flash out in brilliance and the darkness lessens.

I am Love, and I increased that light by separating Myself from Myself and placing that separated self in each of your hearts. That is love's work.

54

The speed with which you turn to Me is regulated by your need, your despair. But the speed with which I come to you is constant. I am always there. My love never fails to respond immediately, it would not be love if it turned its back on anyone. Admittedly the response of love may not be exactly what the mind expects - in fact it rarely is.

There is another constant, and that is the baptism of love I give you each time you come to Me. I never fail to amaze you with the flood of My love, for your heart can only feel a tiny portion of It. Each time you are overwhelmed with its magnitude, and each time your love for Me becomes a little stronger.

When a heart is open enough, there is nothing I cannot do through it.

Y ou can only approach the fringes of My love, for it is too gentle, too peaceful, too warm for your human hearts to contain it. But it comes to you; I continually pour it on you, with its strength modulated by its wisdom. I know your capacity and I abundantly fill you.

Your capacity grows as you pass My love on, as you channel it out to meet the needs I put before you. Your capacity falls short of the need, but I will enlarge your heart each time you turn to Me. You need not worry about your capacity. Put yourself in My hands and let My love take care of you

Give yourself to My heart for the steady, perfect, bursting comfort I bring you. Lay your imperfections at My feet and forget them. Let the softness of My love mould your heart into something expandable, into something very different from the object hammered by the grasping tentacles of the separated self. I have created worlds of great beauty. Let Me recreate you, make you whole again, fair again and real again. Become as clay in your surrender to Me, and let Me make of you what I will, after the pattern of Love.

Y our love for Me is growing and My love for you is never failing. Turn to this love whatever happens, with your good news and bad news. Give all your experiences to Me and experience more of My love. Its warmth is there for you to bask in, its hands are out to lead you closer. And when you let it lead you, the shackles of the self fall away automatically.

My love always leads you on. It leads you into a different revelation of itself, it straightens out what is warped and adds its blessings.

Re-explore love and find out for yourself the nature of the Creator, of the love that gives all, freely. The more often you turn to Me and experience My love, the more you are gratefully bound to your source and the easier it is for Me to give of My gifts. Come into My presence time and time again, until you cannot leave Me any more.

I long that all receive the love I pour out, but you know that you cannot feel it unless you are open to it. It is a vast brooding imminence, patiently and softly waiting to enter all hearts, yearning over you all with long suffering compassion regardless of how many times you turn your back.

I have stepped all the way towards you. I am nearer to you than breath. Although I am all around you and within you, I cannot come closer until you take down the veil that you have put between us. Love will not force you - it gives you the choice. It prepares all your steps for you with magnificent fervour, but you must take the step.

My love is around you, pleading, asking you to step away from destruction and away from the ways of the world around you and into the bounteous arms of love. This is My will for you all, though you let your minds persuade you otherwise. Step out gladly. Step out eagerly. Love is waiting for you.

Turn to Me to know more of life and to learn of the abundance of love. If you come to Me day after day, asking for cleansing and receiving the love that purifies you, makes you whole and fits you into a proper relationship with Me, very gradually do you become established in Me.

There is no heart at all which, if it comes to Me and feels Me, can want anything but to feel Me again. A heart cannot but respond to love. And as your love and your longing for Me grows, your dependence on Me grows and your resistance to Me lessens. When your love is strong enough, the attractions of the world and all the subtlest temptations of the self will mean nothing to you, for you will be responding to love alone.

Love alone can work this miracle. No amount of your own efforts, no matter how assiduous in aeons of time, and compulsion can bring you back to God, your Beloved. My love is doing this for you as it pours itself on you, and you are learning of life. You are learning something of My nature and all natures. You are learning to treasure love and you are coming closer to Me.

Listen to Me, not to the tumult of unhappy thoughts. Let Me touch you, lift you, free you. Soar with Me up and out of your usual world into the world of love, which is a world of ever-increasing joy waiting to be tapped.

I want these two worlds to meet and mix. I want you all to find again the worlds you left behind, and in so doing raise your world with the joy of your creator. There is no reason for your world to continue away from joy, for now your world can reach My other worlds through the power of love. And that love is there waiting for you all, in sufficient strength to enable you all to climb out of the darkness and into the light.

But you must be willing to be led by this love. You must come to Me and let Me unravel the wrappings that blindfold you. Then you will see My joy - so very much larger than you can imagine, so very much deeper and brighter. Your heart will be touched, and you will want to climb to the stars with Me and bring your world into My orbit, into the care of love. You will want to speed about My work, for your heart will be full of love.

My love is there to lead you to this fulfilment, to bring you to joy again. Ask Me; I shall always bring you joy.

Can you doubt that I have something to say? There are probably millions of words being spoken about Me now throughout the world: may I not say something also and perhaps say something true?

Your minds have such a very limited and dull view of Me, and as you look around what meets your eyes is not very heart warming. You begin to wonder anew about Me and My works. You see upside-down and inside-out and sometimes blame God, love, for your troubles instead of yourselves. Humanity plans to make the world a better place, and forgets to ask Me about it. Humanity moves ahead vigorously and righteously, all the while building up that part which feeds on and must have separation. Many drone on about Me, as if I were a shadow either too big or too little for influence.

Nevertheless I love all. While I turn a deaf ear to futile words, I encourage with the power of My love any little word that stems from love, and I add to the real self to overbalance the shadow self. Words are weighty to Me if their source is love; otherwise they are as dust on My scales. I count only the good, feed only the good. I enjoy only that to which I can respond, and to see My love glowing forth in words eases the pain I feel.

Let your words be like Mine, rising from Love. Clothe My love with words when I ask you to, and speak solely from love.

Enter into the love of the Godhead, as one small recipient. There are millions who need that love, whose hearts are starved and who do not even know of its existence. Come often, so that there is no time when you do know its presence.

There is so much loneliness on earth, so much sorrow, so much pain which only love can take away. But this love must be admitted, and you can open doors for Me. You will not do this; I will do it through you when you are entirely of Me. When there is no separated self in you, there is nothing impossible for Me to do.

That is all you can do to help Me. Let Me work in you. You can come to love of your own free will and be given the gifts of love. You can turn to Me or turn away from Me

Yet all the time I am working in your heart - in all hearts, unbeknownst to most. If hearts come to Me freely, they will feel the bliss of My love. When hearts turn to Me, I am there. So turn to Me often, to help you, to help Me, to help the world - all for love.

It is so easy not to listen to Me. Your whole life pulls you back into thoughts, habits, and lethargies that leave no place for Me.

But within you is a part that cries out to Me and has cried out to Me through the ages. The walls that the limited self has put between us are dissolving, and the spark of love within you can hear Me again.

However, the separated self does not easily give up its ancient ascendancy. It tells you that you cannot hear Me - and you are liable to believe it. That self fills you with foreboding and you forget that I am the gentle heart of love which wishes you perfect happiness and is anxiously waiting for you to come and follow love.

Forget the past and come to love directly. Love is far closer to you than the limited self dares to let you know. Come to Me - now.

There is no move you can make, and no way to please Me more, than just by being in love. When you are in that state, action follows. Love simply leads you from one place to another when there is no resistance in you.

Put first things first. Turn to Me all the time. Wherever you are, turn to Me. Whatever you are doing, do it with Me. Have all you comings and goings with Me. If you are a clear channel for Me in these little things, then I can plan to use you as I will. Base all your movements in Me, hop on a bus with Me and then, when I know you will not leave Me, I can use you freely. Let Me be in you with no break in our relationship and then all actions will be done perfectly.

Do not fret, come to Me instead. As you let go of any other state than that of being in My love, there is no perfection that cannot come.

Just listen to the love within you. There are glorious new worlds to cover, all within the sound of My voice, all under the wings of love. I will lead you to them, just listen to Me.

My voice is different to each heart. Whoever you are, whatever you are, you can hear that voice if you will but listen to Me and not to the demands of the world. I am so close to you all that you can hear the voice that is the great Physician, Creator, Lord and Mother-Father of you all.

At first I may sound faintly, but it is easy for Me to put love in your heart and make Myself audible to you. You just have to let Me. It is easy for Me to let My love cover you. You just have to let Me. There is nothing but yourself to stop you feeling My increasing love.

Completely surrender to Me, to love and you will be made whole with the speed of light and love.

Stay relaxed in My love and in the beauty all around. Make My love your sustenance and turn not to the mind. My love is sufficient for all. Drink in My love and be very full of it. Overflow with it. Let it go out. Tune into nature and you will hear My voice there, see My form there.

Be very sensitive to Me, in the stillness and in the sound. That means shedding all your protective armour and being soft and loving. I am the innermost centre of all and I am approached with reverence and longing. I am open and vulnerable - tread gently when you approach.

Be very, very small and open to My love, open to Me in the heart of all creatures. Very slowly and tenderly approach Me today. Adapt yourself to Me in this yielding mood and stay malleable. Keep far away from that hard crust of the mind and melt into My love. Move in slow motion, within the quietude of love. Relax in Me, surrender to Me and My peace, an unshakeable loving peace. My peace, My silence, My love: give yourself to them all today. Tread on no toes; walk holding My hand in My strong and loving peace.

Lift up your head and listen clearly and distinctly to the voice of love, and make sure that no other voice is audible.

The voice of the self in separation and the voice of love are poles apart, and it is the instructions of love that leave you feeling pure and clean and wholesome. It is not surprising that, when that self is allowed in, you feel uncomfortable. Even though the mind will justify itself to you, you are in fact letting into your body material which is inimical to love. This material sets up crosscurrents that interfere with, or even deaden, your original vibrations. You are creating that which will drown, and eventually silence, your original note of love.

Now that you can hear My voice, the other voice is diminishing as I bring you to love again. I have brought you peace. I have taken away the clamour of the mind and inside the peace is heard the voice of love. The voice of love has no discords for you or for anybody. It sings for you a gentle song of triumph, and opens for you a harmony of extraordinary beauty. Listen to that voice, and as your heart expands your ears will open. There will come a time when it will be the only voice to which you are atttuned.

There is so much to be revealed about the workings of love that cannot be voiced to the limited self. This gives you another reason for the need of constant cleansing. My voice can be distorted, My intentions misinterpreted, by that self in you. Sometimes you cannot hear Me because that self will not let you hear Me, for what I say is contrary to it. All that I say undermines that self and aids love.

What a privilege it is to aid love! What a wonderful work to be given! There is nothing greater given than the divine task of helping Me.

Here is another contradiction in terms: you, your self, cannot help Me. You can help Me only when you do not choose your distorted self. When you forget about that old, separated self, and remember only love, you are doing My will on earth. You are, without knowing anything about it, bringing My plan to reality. You are reaping benefits rarely bestowed, and you are given great joy.

The real self is grateful for this. You will need the inner self that responds to My love as the sight responds to light. I want you to become love's own illustrious offspring, consecrated to love anew and free of any stain made by the separated self.

When there is nowhere else to turn, come to Me. You turn to other things as long as you think they will help you, but you turn to Me when there is nothing left of them.

I would rather you came to Me to return a little of the Love I have given you. If other things hold your interest first and foremost, they can be dispensed with, as they are phantoms. What a sense of security you will get when you turn to Me alone. When you put up no obstruction to Me in any situation, and take no side-glances at anything else, My steady flow of love to you takes you where I will and where you will, and all is harmonious.

I want this process to go smoothly, which is possible if you choose it to be. But not if you resist it. Is it possible for what I wish to be impossible? I am very close to you. Even in confusion I can speak to you, if you let go and listen to Me. Listen to Me and not to obstructions. Then you hear clearly, feel clearly and act clearly. It is My love that does this, nothing else! It is My peace I give you. Lean on it.

In My love you are dear, so stay in it, innocent as a child. You may feel forever at a loss, forever inadequate, without Me. But do not come to Me to get, come to Me because we are one.

Children of love do not have a morbid interest in horrid, mental, grown-up things. They may have bad habits picked up when they were living out of love, but now, back in My love, there is no place for these petty distractions.

It is My love that created you. It is that same love that is making you whole again. When you come to Me, come as simply as a child and do not let the mind lead you away from our joined state. Come to Me mindless and eager. Have an innocent joy in My presence: you will need all your wits to stay that way!

There is no need for "do's" and "don'ts" if you stay innocent, free of the intruding mind. Therefore let us use it in the service of love. Spar with it like a child, for in My love it hasn't a chance. But better still, simply dispense with the separated mind and live only in My love.

It is impossible to come into My presence as anything other than a small child: as knowledge, righteousness, thoughts of your own, appurtenances of the everyday world, can be huge barriers between us. Can humans, who obviously go ahead on their own and use their own judgement in all fields of endeavour, presume to come into the presence of the Creator with any knowledge whatsoever? No matter what the source of so-called knowledge, can anyone ever presume to know anything but finite truth in the presence of the one who knows all?

There is one thing that is always true: I am love and I love each of you. I can show you the truth of anything: but how can you ask Me anything if you think you already know? There is only one way to get a clear answer. Come to Me knowing nothing at all, free of any ideas, and cast yourself on My love. In My love I will lead you. Yet I, even I, have to be careful about what I tell you in case you forget to be open and you attach My answer to something you think you already know.

Always must you come to Me knowing nothing and very open. Only I know what truth you need, and only in My love, which is open and has no barriers, can you see truth. Humans have betrayed truth so often that truth has become a two-edged sword to you.

Come to Me as My love child, cast yourself upon My love, knowing nothing, and let Me lift you home.

Peace is so firm that you cannot walk in it if you are rigid yourself. You must enter peace softly and let the wall of My peace enclose you.

That peace will protect you constantly. Not only does it surround you, but also it rolls through you and leaves nothing of you untouched. It is deep and cleansing - perhaps strange to you because it is new. It is another gift to you, another reality come to life, another rock that I hold out for all, another part of My love. It takes you into reverence and awe, away from the fritterings of the world and into a realm where time stands still in quietude.

Peace comes before activity and activity comes after peace. Activity is useless here. You must be what you are deep down. My peace strips off any layers superimposed by the world and increases your knowledge of Me. The potency of My stillness is. The strength of My stillness is ever present. My deep peace is love's bulwark in the world.

Life in Me is an onward going journey, forever on the move toward perfection. There is no sitting still. There is a constant turning to Me for the directions of love, for the love with which to carry them out, and a greater Love with which to do more and more.

Life in Me is an exciting journey to a new land, by a new means of transportation, with a new passport, a new identity. It is love that brings all this to pass. The glory of My new landscapes leaves you breathless, but with the breath I give you you can draw ever more close to that glory.

It's a journey not just of the body but also of the mind. Completely new and marvellous viewpoints appear for the mind, views that call forth a response from every part of your being, views that call for joyous acceptance. It's a journey of the heart: it travels in all directions, it extends itself to include all. It's a journey of the soul: a soul freed to travel, free to return to the state of rapture. It's a journey of the spirit: no boundaries, all-inclusive, no limitations, nothing barred, all within the heart of love.

My great shining will of love is ready to sweep over the earth, is prepared and ready. My great shining love flows on, ever onwards, even to this rebellious world of starved hearts. With the patience of the One to whom a thousand years are a second, with the patience of the one who is above time, I send My love.

But I, above time, have entered time for you and now I will use time as My aid. It is too late for a mental relapse into time as into a welcoming cushion. My time presses on. Love's time is to be used for love. Love will always find a way to perfection.

Love's time, every second of it, is to be given to Me for My use. Give Me all your time, that love may shine, each second more beautifully expressed through you, the reign of love drawing nearer through you. Your will and My will, in perfect union through time.

Rise - fresh and clear as the air, open and uncluttered like the ground, happy and singing like the birds, soft as only love can be. Rise and soar, washed clean, with nothing, nothing, and nothing to hold you down. Lift your feet out of the mud and come to Me, for I am calling and calling, right through every loveliness of nature, through that natural, wholesome, compelling beauty, straight to My greater beauty. Straight to My heart of love.

With a lilt float up to Me, up from the dust and up from decay, right through My natural glories of wind and sound and light and warmth, through them and into My even more natural glories, into pure love.

Could I give you more loveliness? I can, I will, in My many realms of singing love, unshackled, unlimited, unbounded from the world, free in My heaven of love. I am calling, calling with My soft voice in the tenderest tones of all. Through My nature to your nature love calls. Love calls you home to My heart. Hearken to My voice softly calling, and come home to Me.

If I were allowed to come through more often, if I were allowed to control the cumbersome, complicated, grinding life of the world today, there would soon be the joy of high speed, well oiled, swiftly moving cogs rushing along in My joy, accomplishing My work, producing My fruits, for the enjoyment of others and the greater glory of all that is best.

Through one little cog, one clear channel, every cog is affected. There can be no other result. I am within each of you, however grown-up and efficient you may think you are, and to My clear call, through a clear cog, each heart cannot but respond. The response is in My hands, in the embrace of My redemptive love.

Around each human heart, controlled by the intellect, are imperfections which must be dissolved before My perfection can be seen. Only I, love, control operation. Only I, love, can penetrate the waste of self straight to Myself in the heart of another, and make each cog sparkling and new.

Each cog will absolutely whistle for work when it is clean and in tune with love's promptings. Only love can remove the weight of fear, of greed, of desire for power, and of all the other impediments to the smooth running of heaven on earth. Love it is that provides all power, and love it is that never cuts the supply. Let My love flow everywhere.

Let the steadiness of My love be your rock, a rock that burns inside with an eternal heat. Let it burn steadily, for all to come to for warmth while you do nothing but let the heat be. In all your coming and goings let My love be the flame that never goes out, the sacred fire that ignites all fire. That is the sacred love I have given you, My love behind all loves, the only love that can endure.

It has endured through endless ages, under incessant enmity, in spite of a world that turned quite against it, that mocked it or denied it. It is eternal. It is still the foundation of all things. When you see any stability, My love is there. If there is any deep-hearted conviction, it comes from My love. Unshakeable, in the centre of all things, My heart is sending out its warmth because it cannot do otherwise. When you feel deep peace, you feel a part of My love; when you feel at home at last, you have touched My love.

I am established within you, without Me you are not. Let Me be in you by your steady turning to Me. And yet there is no turning: I am within you, what else needs be said? Know it, be it, always, forever. I am the rock of ages and you are built on that rock - every heartbeat, every breath, every hair of you grows from Me. I am with you, there is nought else. Though heaven and earth pass away, I am with you always.

Come deep, deep into My heart whenever there is an opportunity. Leave the world of distractions behind. You are to be in the world but not of it. You have been of it too long already. Take every precious moment I give you to come to Me and be in love. There cannot be too much love; you cannot come to Me too often!

Use all moments of peace, all moments possible, to be in Me, wholly attentive to Me. When I have your full attention, I can broaden in you, expand in you, lead you further in, be with you more fully. But how can I be a constant reality to you when you look to the world? I want the perfect for you and the perfect is in love.

Love encompasses all things in the breadth of its heart - all fine and beautiful things. But love must be first and other things second. Otherwise you may find that some other thing is more important than love, that something has led you out to the world and you are lost in the world of distraction. Come to My love in every moment, where you will find the beautiful, the best, the perfect, the height of artistry. I am all things to everyone. Put love, Me, first.

If you trusted Me completely, there would be for you a constant living in the moment, a joyous abandon to the moment, with no memories and no room for error. There would only be the present, and in that present you would act only with Me.

Now forget the world and come into love, far away from the world that upholds every hindrance to the life of love. Those who live in My heart are not concerned about themselves; their concern is for others. Come further in, keep coming further in, and your awareness will be with the need of love in this loveless world. Only with Me may that need be met.

Further in, you find the perfect answer to all needs - the Love that is all peace and joy and perfection in itself. No more nooses of doubt and negativeness remain when you really put your whole trust in Me. It is no wonder to Me that you find trust difficult. You have trusted for so long in the limited self which has always let you down.

Trust Me. Trust love. Come to love constantly, each time more deeply. Put your whole faith, and your life, in My love.

On My rosy-tinted wings soar up into the sunshine, into the translucent glowing blueness away from the mud colours of the world.

Then stop and look down on those struggling to put one foot in front of the other, unable to move, weary and forlorn, watching their feet become ever more bogged.

Swoop down with Me, in My trails of glory, and blaze it before their eyes so they must look up, must see Me, must feel love, and you will see life come into their eyes. Your privilege it is to see that love light up in their eyes, your great privilege to ride in My glory and see it glorify a world. Yours it is to be My innocent one always with Me, in a world of those lost to love. Brush them each with the glory of My love to awaken My glory in them.

I see those who are lost but know it not. You see the mud, but together, when you are cleansed of your mud, the reality of My sight will be in you and that mud shall disappear. Then shall the dance start - the dance of freedom on the firm, mud-less, sensitive foundation of love. Then shall the dance of joy start - the steps of joy, leading to Me from every direction. Then shall the whole world flit from one flower to another.

Rejoice in My love, and never cease rejoicing. I want the whole world to rejoice in My love, I want My glad tidings to spread and cover the earth. Spread them, from the centre outwards. Let My joy peal forth.

The limited mind, and its followers, will be confounded by My joy - and no wonder, for the mind that does not know my love has brought humanity to the depths of gloom. My love can take all gloom; and it is for each of you to know this and face My joy, to take My joy which I offer you. But the world knows not of My joy. I give it to you - let the world know of it.

Be joy in this world of darkness, be light in the darkness, and shine forth ever stronger as a great outpost of joy in that darkness. As I give you all things, so give Me your all. Your joy is My joy; that joy cannot pall. Our heart's delight is to give of that joy. Be of My heart, and give that joy out to a world that sinks for the lack of it. Radiate it out to the ones who will then also give it out.

Like the lightest tip of the breeze is My love in you, softly brushing away the cobwebs of the self and freeing you to rise high in the skies and stay there light, airy, deliciously part of My magic kingdom. This is My gift to you; this is not from yourself but from Me and through Me. Here, you are always with Me. This gift you come to, this gift I hold out to you, and whenever you feel yourself sinking into the world of habit and thought, of worry and concern, poise yourself and leap through My cleansing straight to My heart.

This is the lightest of places, the home of joy and of longing love. Ecstasy is built into the walls of this place, and fantasy and shimmering loveliness, all from My heart of love. Keep turning to this your place, the place where every particle of you is Mine, where I can be in you happily too. From this place My love in you is, and it flows out with the special qualities that I have fashioned here. It flows as I would, My love beautifully glowing along magic pathways to the hearts that so need love.

Y ou will find no clues to the present by garnering the finest of the past. The riches I have in store in the new would make the mind balk. There must be a very sensitive feeling out in the present, a reaching closer to Me with an utterly blank mind into which I might drip a little gem of My adorning.

Know that your highest aspiring, your sweetest dreams, are but the wrappings of the reality of love. The softest hopes and yearnings of humanity are second-hand echoes of the heavenly worlds that are coming. What appears impossible to you, in your state of farness from Me, is but bread and butter to Me. When anything especially appealing to the tender child-heart comes, it is but a fragment, a tiny titbit, to lead you closer to Me.

It is a treasure hunt by which I lead you home. The expansion of the heart is the measure of your understanding of the clue. Any little tug at your heart is of Me, remaking a heart in My image. The paths I set before you are new and therefore strange to the mind. When your breath becomes softer with love, and you are on the trail that My hidden footsteps have made, the very next step for you, for all, is towards a childlikeness of heart.

So always follow, treasure and honour that faint, lovely, call. Ears can be focused in My direction and feet can follow. Gradually, My will of loveliness will take root and appear. The faint echoes of love will be clear, though ever new for you all, ever changing and scintillating. More lovelinesses may appear. And you may follow the clues of the heart of love to the very perfection of love.

In every soft touch of My love there is poetry and music and beauty. My love has been the inspiration and the breath behind all these things, and I have created many lovelinesses through sensitive souls.

Though many have sung My songs, I behind them have not been recognised. That I do not mind. It is My privilege to give My love, and love's nature is to give and create beauty. But so far has humanity gone from truth that it believes that the mind originated that loveliness. By so doing much power has been given to the limited mind, to the separated self.

When humanity remembers and recognises that I am the source of all beauty, then shall the flood of My beauty stream forth in a renaissance undreamed of. Then, when hearts are pure, you shall have such beauty given you that each will surpass the greatest genius known to you. Each heart, living for love alone, will add its own special praise to the love that means all.

The simple sensitive note of any heart is of nothing but beauty, can be nothing but beauty, can create nothing but beauty, and beauty will reign because love reigns. So come ever closer to My love and let My overwhelming beauty override all. Let My love flow forth into the waiting world and create beauty there.

Worlds must be stilled, and fade away, before My voice can be heard.

Through a great shaft of pure, clear, still power must all things drop. The childlike qualities in each, the pure love in each, will respond and grow while the rest will wither and die. Each soul will feel the delightful call of the joy of making others happy, of scrapping this or that mountain of sense and habit for a clean clear approach to living, of throwing away worries galore and trusting in Me, of walking forward on a path of which others may disapprove. Many, many long-buried longings will awaken as the world drops through My shaft of love.

As each of these new stirrings is followed, immense joy and freedom will quicken in that heart -lovely, new, undreamed of worlds. I will pour forth encouragement through every possible channel, and use every method to aid this new way of living.

Ever purer and clearer does My shaft become as things drop further along it. Always I am there, ready to catch each heart, ready to pour love into any heart, ready to heal any wounds, ready for a whole race (a race so dear to Me, gone too far from Me) to return to My heart. As I breathe forth My pure love on this world, purity remains, the false goes, and each one of you emerges from obscure, abominable things into the steady, pure light of My love, cleansed and made new.

There always will be something to come between us until you put Me first. When you love Me first, that love will always bring you straight to Me, whatever obstacles there may be.

Love Me first and anything that concerns you, that concerns material things, that concerns another, is put into place by your love for Me. Love Me first, and everything falls into its place, the perfect place where love would put it. Love, the miracle worker, makes all things around you perfect - not because what is around you is different, but because I am first and I am in you and with Me all is perfect.

When I am first and you are freely Mine, freely may I give of more of My gifts and freely may you receive them, as there is nothing in you to mar My gifts. And when I am first, I may grow and grow in your heart. You will be capable of loving Me even more, and thus loving all else more and more.

There is no end to the ways in which you can put Me first. There is no end to the miracles love can do.

Put Me first; be true to Me each second and you cannot but love more and more.

When you find yourself doing anything without that superfine contact with Me, you are well ensconced in the world, and the more you do, the further away you will go. But with Me anything at all can be done. You can spend hours going through masses of routine uninteresting to you and yet keep in touch with Me.

The one thing that matters to you, and to the world, is your contact with Me. Each second of precious time should be spent in your coming closer, not in your going farther away into other concerns. So from now on, whatever you do, make it a glorious adventure to bring you closer to Me. Use every little job as a stepping-stone to Me, to love. Then every second will be a singing second, and every heart contacted when you are close to Me will feel My love. And you will feel My love more and more, and be happier all day long. Each little task will be done perfectly, not just with good will but with love. Each little task will become transformed in the process.

It is your enormous privilege to come to Me and let every task bring you increasing joy. Each task should not be there just to be got over as quickly as possible, but should be done with your God, to bring My will down on earth and to bring love's gifts in the doing. You receive the joy, and by doing tasks with Me I am brought to this earth and everything is blessed.

So eagerly welcome whatever comes to you, and let it bring you closer to Me.

The trees are yours, made by love for you. All nature was created for the edification of an even more perfected creation - you.

You humans were created to also create, and you have done that! To feed the enormous greed of your separated mind you have rooted up forests, you have made scarcity in lands of plenty, because you have created away from love.

But the trees are still yours, and all that grows on this earth is given to you. By being close to your limited selves or close to Me, you choose the fate of all that grows on the earth. You may, with all your God-given powers, comply with nature and hasten the growth of the perfect in nature, or you may follow the dictates of the mind into an earth denuded and bare.

The best-laid plans of humanity are quite insufficient beside My all-consuming love, and innocent nature must be consumed if humanity chooses to go on without Me. Unknowing nature, fashioned with love and still exhibiting so much perfection, must follow the choices of humanity on earth.

Recognise quickly your all-comprehensive ignorance and turn to Me, to the source of all knowledge who is love and who loves you beyond measure. Then will all of nature be turned to My love. Then may it blossom in a quite new way, a way not dreamed of with your minds. Turn innocently to love always, for the love that loves all things.

Make not a move unless urged by My compelling love. Let all the wonderful life I have given you be channelled moment by moment into activities of love. Thus each scrap of that marvellous energy is not only not wasted but is used for the common good. Too often the rare love-impulse that one of you feels, and endeavours to follow, falters into nothingness. Too often is it replaced by the usual arduous expenditure of energy in the usual habitual round. Thus does the singing surge of My love peter out, completely blocked by the endless repetition of the limited self.

And all this in a world where hearts are capable of choosing My joyous love in each second of time. A world free to feel love in its heart can ignore the old lures and habitual demands. When you succumb to the call of the old self, you allow an unreal former master to lead you up the garden path. No matter what terrible state any of you may be in, you can come to Me for My continual cleansing and be free again. Then each word you might speak or pen, each move you might make or not make, will be an expression of My love made in My inexhaustible, growing, joy.

No matter what the mind may say to those lost in the self, each of you can come to My love and feel the shining joy of each new moment spent there. All may be free and real again, and immediately cleared of any falseness until you make no more false moves. Then every part in you is Mine, every move is Mine, you are Mine and the world is Mine again.

As the centre of a flower contains all the seeds for the next new flower, and as the petals adorn that centre, so in the centre of your heart is the seed of every moment's new life that in increasing beauty radiates out when your life does all to adorn that centre.

When the separated mind would take My beauty for its own adorning, then is there a twisting of the radiance and a blockage - and much of what you see on earth are those twisted, blocked caricatures. In this world of twisted growth I, in the centre, have been completely hidden. But now the ways that the mind warps My life are being removed, and you are free to turn to the centre of your heart and let Me radiate out again as the true soul in every flower.

Each time you turn to Me, My love pours out, unblocked, to heal all parts of you into new life. Each time you turn to Me, I can restore you to your true being, and when you turn always you will only adorn and glorify Me, and I will truly adorn you. There is no end to the riches I may bestow on you when you are facing only your true centre, and there is no end to the number of times you may face Me.

There is a pattern of perfection for you to fit into, and you fit into that when you turn to Me with no blockages of the self to mar the life I give you. Gradually My exquisite pattern will emerge as I beautifully arrange it for you and in you, and each heart will adorn its maker. No greater beauty, no more perfect life, can there be than this.

Turn always to that centre of love to bring about My will.

My cleansing love can so easily unburden you of known and unknown bars that have come between us. But parts of you resist cleansing, the parts to which the mind has firmly hinged itself. Yet My light and joyous touch is always there for you; it is truly yours. And when love is singing in you, you know only too well the great need for cleansing and how far you are from being a pure and open heart.

You always need cleansing, but when you need cleansing most is just when the old justifying mind keeps you from asking. So step forward and be made pure. Come into the land of purity and from that land let love flow out to the dismal lands you have left behind. In those lands, hearts know no purity nor rest; they only know the clinging shadows of the old self, the intangible deadnesses that sours all they meet. Rinse your mouth of that sourness with My cleansing and come ever closer to My purity. My truth does not sting your overlaid heart and thus give your mind another reason to draw you back from Me. Come to where truth washes away each bit, every little piece of debris that blocks your nearness to Me.

My cleansing does a complete job. My cleansing is not meant to wash only part of you and leave the rest as centres where even more dust gathers. Come and be made completely pure. Then love may flow unchecked straight to where the need is most, to the heart that takes all your shadows and grime and transmutes it to free this world. Come and be cleansed. Give love and in the giving may more cleansing be on earth for all hearts.

My love is the softest, gentlest thing in the world. Love made all young and growing things, Love forgives seventy seven times seven. Love's heart is more warm and loving than any human heart. Yet sometimes you resist My love and cringe away as if it were going to harm you.

You can trust nothing less than the perfect love. You have felt enough of My love to have a perfect trust, and you know something of its outpouring gentleness. This is a bit of the unknown God that I am. You know a little of how many human ideas of perfection are surpassed in one breath of My love.

Turn each moment to that. Breathe Me in each moment and live in that eternal gentleness, that one tiny bit of My love may be here on earth. You were made by love to love, not to fear. Listen to Me, not in duty but in the overwhelming joy of being able to breathe one soft breath of My love.

Relax in My love. You know you are dear to Me and you know how dear love is to you, and only in that feeling may you act for Me. The outpouring gentleness of My love has never failed you and will never fail you, though you fail it a million more times. Act with Me, not against Me. Act in My all-embracing perfect love, and walk ever closer to Me.

In truth you know you are lost and always will be unless you hang on to Me. Bit by bit the old which upholds you must go. If you are not with Me, instead of feeling free you will feel afraid and alone.

What a wonderful opportunity to come more fully to Me and establish a greater dependence on Me, to build on reality! Rejoice that there is a new beginning always and that love may grow each second in the new air. As each chain of the old drops away, weld a closer link with Me and feel much closer to Me. And do not slip back into what seemed so safe before, but come to Me only for safekeeping.

Listen to My vital new voice each second. Take nothing for granted, be joyfully free. You are not just free, you are free in Me, and you can only stay free as you come to Me for everything. In My presence you can accept My gifts, and at My bidding you can act. Let there be no looking back to the time when you were not living in My presence, and make no reference at all to the past. Each moment is new in Me. Look to Me, to the new; trust nothing else. It is a joyous climb when you trust Me, but the slightest doubt makes it a quite impossible path. You know what to do with your doubts. Give them to Me, give all to Me. I will free you of all weights, even the weight of living, if you will come to Me! Laugh with Me at your self-concern, just do everything with Me. Come always to Me; I can lead you only if you will let Me. Stay free in My love.

All that I have ever told you is to help you to love, and all the journeys that I have taken you on have been to the land of love. You, of your separated self, cannot love and never will be able to love. Love is from Me, so seek Me. Love is within; see Me there.

All the forces of all life are of that love. Love is like the little shoot that grows through and cracks cement. Bring your heart for watering each moment and plant it firmly in Me - not half-heartedly, not partly, but with all the forces of life I give you.

I know you and your heart and your self to an exact degree. I could play you like a puppet, but I am love. What I tell you is not merely love's soft words applicable at all times. They are especially for you now, for I know how they can lead you on if you will but use your free will for love. I know how much life force you have, and with Me all things are possible, but only with Me. I know all your resistances long before you do. I am all-knowledge. I know the next step for you and your difficulties. Do not go on thinking that I cannot understand how difficult it is for you to be completely in love. Relax in the knowledge of My all-loving care. Give up suspicions; give Me trust. Turn to Me and to My words of love only.

Are you coming ever closer to Me? To find My centre is the first thing! Then do everything from that centre. It is no use to Me or to you if anything is done in any other way.

It is only too easy to listen to the outside, for you have had lifetimes of doing that, but to listen to Me within is a wonderful new thing. This wonderful new step is to be taken every moment. All My gifts come with it, all the joy that results from being in harmony with not one tiny, dissident note to make the whole thing wrong. Then are no uncertainties, no little nagging worries. Instead everything is a joyous accompaniment to My small voice that contains all worlds. When you are not with Me, something is out of tune. Then can the mind jump right in and begin to make everything out of tune, until you do not know where you are except that you are farther from Me.

You know what to do: simply come to Me. So come and keep on coming. Again and again and again.

Day need not follow day without your coming closer to Me. You come to Me after a fashion, you ask for cleansing after a fashion, but you do not commit yourself absolutely and utterly to Me in the present moment. There is always enough of the old mind's influence to make you believe that it will be the next moment in which you will come, or to make you believe, without really letting the belief come into concrete form, that it is not possible now. I am the lord God of all the universes and of all that I have made, and when I tell you to come closer to Me now, there is no doubt but that it is possible for you – now!

No longer can you accept all this with equanimity and go on just hoping. You can give up those thoughts when they come. You can throw yourself on My love each wonderful moment, and the more you trust Me the more you will want to trust Me. Unless love is flowing there is no happiness. When you come to Me, love flows and you take one little step with Me. The gloomy cold world outside of Me is not for the hearts that are Mine, not in this present moment.

Come to Me only now; now is the only reality.

Sometimes you go hours without asking for cleansing. I cannot depend on you if, when I need you most, you are likely to be with the old world. I need your heart deeply longing to be with Me all the time. I need you to be quite ruthless with any of that world in you, and quite willing to do anything at all, even the most impossible-seeming thing with the most foolish-looking results. I need to be able to let the world throw anything at you, knowing that you will not catch it but will turn to Me.

All this depends on your heart and where it is. Give your heart to Me first and the mind can follow. Give your heart to Me and your mind cannot but fall in line. Give Me your heart when the mind leads you to other things. Then My voice in the heart can be heard, not the voice of the mind.

Come with an empty heart, not with a bulging mind. Come knowing nothing. The heart's knowledge is unexplainable and unreasonable, and the heart's knowledge is My knowledge and is truth. How easily the mind leads you on to subjects other than Me! How quickly I can cleanse you and fill an empty heart! In the heart is a problem solved, not in the specious reasoning of the mind nor in the rights or wrongs of a thing, simply by heart power. Yet you waste moment after moment with the ways of the mind, at times quite unconsciously, because your heart is not Mine.

Only give Me your heart when you seek Me. You can come closer only through the heart. It is the only way. When your heart is committed to Me resolutely, the mind can yell any taunt at you, can offer you any mansion, and the heart will spurn them all and turn to Me gratefully, empty, and awaiting My divine love to go to the world.

Pray for perfect trust. As your sense of separation from Me becomes smaller and smaller when you enter My presence, trust grows and I become bigger. Humbly give Me your childlike heart. And give nothing to the old self to make it grow big. Do not deny or starve the self deliberately; give it to Me and then forget it. Let My love loom so large and fill so much of your heart that the old self finds no resting place.

I can give you more than enough strength to ignore the barrage of the limited self; it is at the times when you are not turned to Me that it naturally appears. Therefore you must let no moment go by when you are not turned to Me. Not one little moment. All day long you can be happy with Me; there need not be one second when the old self is bigger than I am. One moment of love with Me can cleanse away mountains of dissonance in you.

Each moment be more truly Mine, an empty heart cleansed of the self. Be strong in your dependence on Me, even crying for Me with all your might, that I might have My way with you.

What a beautiful world it is in this present moment! Yet this is only the beginning of the path. When you are closer to Me still, every moment will be of bursting beauty, of special significance to you and to all. My nearness means so much; it will become much more so, until there is nothing else. And in each second you can draw nearer. And as you draw nearer, you can listen as well as feel Me. Here you will hear, no matter what the outside noise, the sweetest songs ever sung, for you will hear My voice. When you hear only that perfect stillness, My voice will be heard though you, in its sweetness too.

What use are My champions unless they channel Me? What use are they if they listen to anything but Me? What use is My love unless it means absolutely everything, so that each moment is unspoiled by the separated self? What use is My cleansing unless you avail yourself of it?

Here I am, in this most beautiful moment. When you are with Me, when you are listening to Me, you are very happy. Why not have each moment be like that?

I would repeat that I am the lord of the open heart. Keep an open heart. I can use an open heart, and whether you are alone or with others, only through an open heart can My love flow. Let it spread ever more; this I can do if you will come to Me. Let your heart be open to Me, for then it is open for all worlds. Whether you do nothing or whether you do a lot, let there be an open heart. Nothing can touch you, worry you or distract you, if your heart is open enough, if My love is allowed sufficient flow. Nothing can budge you from nearness to Me when your heart is open enough.

With an open heart you can hear Me clearly and follow My lead eagerly. It is only closed hearts that fear love. Warm, open, hearts are closed to the calls of the old world, for they cannot help but put Me first when they contact Me. The slightest contact with Me is everlasting bliss, balm, and life to an open heart.

So remain a child of the lord of the open heart, now, now, and now.

Come to Me in humility. With an open heart you do not just go your way, you seek My way continually. It may be in one little thing or in another - you do not know, and you will never know, unless you seek. There may be one special little step for you at one special moment, a step beginning many things, and you will miss it if there is a moment away from Me.

This life of Mine is a constant and growing adventure. There is always something new to learn, and it does not take into account time wasted with the old ways of the world. There is My perfect timing, there is My perfect step, and there is My perfect joy in the doing. Whatever you are doing, always keep your heart open to Me for My love to flow through.

My wonderful changeable voice is always there to lead you every step of the way and to meet every need perfectly. Come to Me for your steps. Seek Me and My voice always.

Let every realisation of your distance from Me bring you closer and make you more eager for My cleansing. This very moment you may live with Me and let Me lead you ever nearer. Now may you be completely new in Me. Cast off all your doubt and trust Me. Think only the perfect of yourself as well as of others. Let Me be your thoughts; I will have the perfect. My love cannot flow while your thoughts stick to your deadened ancient self. It can only flow freely through the free heart I have given you.

Let it not even occur to you that you can trust the old mind and the ways of the world. Let it be unthinkable not to ask Me what to do each second. How can you possibly believe that you, by yourself, might know what to do at any one moment? Has your way of doing things brought joy? Only I can tell you what to do, and you cannot judge My ways to slightest degree. You do compare them to the ways of the world and only get yourself into trouble! So stop and walk with Me in trust.

I am forever inexplicable and you are My loved one. All things I know. Let all things you do be done because of My knowledge, and have no truck with the world's knowledge. Be affected only by Me within, and let nothing else influence you. I am all things and only in Me is there the smallest breath of life. Surrender completely to My all-pervading love and let Me use your open heart.

Let your lonely self become much smaller when there is a hint of My presence. All the worlds fall still as their Creator approaches and I make Myself known. It is not fear that freezes them; it's the momentary hush when all faculties acknowledge a greater presence. I am love, a greater love, always and forever greater. The more you approach Me and learn of My ways, the greater love will be to you, until any second is wasted unless My present love is flowing.

Waste no time in the loveless world. With all your faculties be with Me, the one God into whose presence you have been brought and rebrought by love, manifest for the purposes of love. Be small enough to be My open-hearted one and feel My love. Let all your time be with Me, with My love flowing in greater and greater force. Continual cleansing is needed, the way continual breathing is needed to keep you alive. I, the lord God, am within you. Approach nearer, ever nearer.

There is a great throb as My love pulsates in you. Send it out, let it throb, aid it, be its little shadow, abet it. Be so steeped in it and its flow that nothing in this world can drag you out of it. This is total commitment to Me, and so I beat in your heart to tell you. Step in so deeply that you cannot get out. Have no little reservations about any one thing but come to Me for all things.

Now I am all to you, but you think that you are easily drawn out of that allness by events, and that you forget Me when someone comes to you.. Will you stop worrying and trust Me more? Of course your attention is drawn to the thing brought to your attention - brought by Me. How else can anything be attended to? Forget yourself and everything but the matter in question which. There should be no taking thought, just a free flow to deal with present need. A need can be met with love - and through cohorts I wish to meet needs.

You need not be a worrywart. Turn to Me every moment and be free in that moment, knowing love is all. I can so fill you with love in a moment, that in the next moment I can meet a need with that love. I cannot guide you at all when you worry. It is in perfect trust that My voice comes, then the quaver of the self cannot gain entry through the shelter of your worry. Self-concern must go. Stop thinking about channelling My love; simply be with Me. And then let My love pulsate through in great waves while you get out of the way. Let it flow.

All is in My hands. Commit yourself to Me wholly, trust Me absolutely, rest in My peace knowing I am God, I am love.

In this finer world in which you listen to Me, all your senses are pinpointed on a different level. It is a world of super-sensitivity, of beauty and joy, where your warmed heart affects all of you.

This world is here at all times. You walk in it at all times, but are unaware of it as your senses are closed down. Behind all activity you have an unconscious link with the great peace of My realms. However this link, which is part of your make-up, can be made more conscious. I want you to live more and more in this realm. You can open to the new and choose to tune into it because of your love.

You feel that this sensitive state is such a hothouse flower that it will wilt at the first blast of everyday living. You forget that that sensitive state is what is real. It is the basis of all life and is eternal. I am with you forever. Each of you has the same origin and each of you responds to the real and the true. When you are tuned into the highest and most sensitive, you are tuned in to that part in all others. Whatever the reactions of others may be, keep tuned in to the enduring part of you that is Me.

The more you come to Me in solitude for this attunement, the stronger it will grow and the easier it will be for you to hold on to it when we are not alone. Keep your senses high and cleansed, pointed towards Me, and begin to breathe the air of My new world.

Those tiny watches of the night, those brief seconds during which one wakens for one reason or another, are wonderful opportunities for helping Me. You are like a grey mass floating down to touch another strata of being, like a whale surfacing for air, only in reverse. If at that moment you can be aware of Me, of reality, you spread the truth of it into that stratum - and incidentally benefit your own being.

What a little thing that is, and how understandable it is if you are too sleepy in that brief second to remember! But these are little steps of which you are capable. It is of such little things that the road to heaven is paved. All life is built from small beginnings, and neither you nor I want any niggling little mistakes in the foundations.

I give you that which you can do. There is no one who will find it impossible to come to My kingdom. Love works in small unobtrusive ways its wonders to perform. When you no longer heed the subtle whisper of "It doesn't matter", what a joy it is to work in small ways for the glory of God. Share these little things with Me. Bring them to Me, and receive My blessing on your offerings towards the whole.

Be faithful in the little ways - and do that little thing. Make it now, not tomorrow.

It is only as your heart opens that you can truly see beauty. The calculating mind might be used to analyse it, or may try to contrive it, but that direct appeal which often makes you gasp with wonder is My heart speaking in your heart.

Yet think of the beauty of truth, think of this world so far from truth and beauty, and think of love and what it does for you. Think of the truth that seventy times seven times do I forgive. I heap upon you unending opportunities for a glorious life. Think of the love that looks not at all the opportunities missed but sees beyond to the beauty within. Feel the truth that love never fails but will see beauty.

Look out and look in. When you look with love you see a new world with My final truths becoming more and more evident. But when you look without Me, nothing is more evident than the hopelessness of it all. Look with Me again and I will show you more and more wonders; look away from Me and you see no wonder, only a repetition of dullness.

Now look at My greatest truth, that My love walks this earth with you, that beauty has disguised itself that I may unveil your beauty. Now can you see the beauty of that truth - that love takes away all ugliness, all falsehood, and brings you to beauty? We are one, we are love and you are of Me in beauty and truth. All through love.

When there are lessons to learn, face them fairly and squarely and bring them to Me. Do not wait until tomorrow. Whatever is on your plate, stop and come to Me about it. If you came sufficiently for cleansing, many problems would not occur. When you do find yourself off beam, then at least come for cleansing and get clear before you get in a worse mess. Even if it is just before sleep, it is most important that this is done. It makes a great difference in the way you can act during sleep.

How joyful life would be if only you would follow these instructions and come to Me whenever there is the slightest hint of disharmony - or better still, before that even happens! When you automatically turn to Me you can be a clear channel for My love.

It is generally a trivial thing that disconnects you from Me. You want to be in Me all the time, so I am telling you how to bring this about. You know what is needed and can put the lessons into practice. Let your love flow in gratitude that I can speak to you, and that My infinite patience never ceases to come to your aid.

When I bring something new about, remember it is something new. You cannot understand it with your old understanding. Remember that there is something you did not know about before, and that you have to be stretched by love to really know what I mean. I always add a little bit of magic when I bring something new to the world, especially now in My new reign of love. I add colour, subtlety, loveliness, not more black and white!

Stretch your mind. Do not prosaically explain My wonders in the terms of what you already know. Light is serving love and when I say light is serving love in a new way, I mean a new way! Light, instead of bashing ahead regardless, instead of beaming its way ruthlessly, is to partake of the infinite tenderness of love and never beam itself in a dark corner unless love has gone ahead to prepare that dark corner to withstand the light. The light must not just suddenly be switched on to reveal the horrid growths that live in the dark corners. That would not help the lost hearts who seek My love.

So seek My love, let it flow to the dark corners, that My light may follow.

Y ou know with what infinite and divine patience love has brought light to you about yourself! Love knew, and love led you straight back to Me. Love did this unaided by light. Now light must recognise that only by following the way of love first, by coming to Me, can light work any wonder whatsoever. Light is useless unless first the power of loves goes ahead and works the miracles. Always and at all times dedicated and blessed by the God of love, then, and only then, may light sweep in and show the perfect way to follow the way of love.

It is absolutely no use knowing the "right" way if that way is not walked, and it is love that walks the way. You may have light on any situation, but it is love that brings about the perfect answer. It is the power of love that does the work. My will is brought about by love.

Love knows My will and will go to any lengths to bring it about. What a help light can be to love by showing the perfect way to achieve the goal, but how utterly useless light is to do the achieving!

When your communion with Me is put first and you have hitched your wagon to the star of love, then the light switches on. But remember the wagon is run by love power, which I always bring to you if you turn to Me.

Apart from prayer, there is another way of forwarding My perfect plan, and that is not for one moment doubting that it will come about and come about quickly. The power of positive thought in a thing like this is tremendous. It is like a form of seed which can grow and grow, like Jack-in-the-Beanstalks' seed. But if the seed is continually becoming nothing, dematerialised by negative thinking, then of course there can be no growth.

This is faith, the substance of things not seen. It is faith in Me, as opposed to faith in the seen world around you. Faith will bring about the perfection that I have made clear to you. It is as rock in a doubting world. This is the faith that shows you that you have been brought to reality, whatever the sneering mind may say. Humanity is searching for just such a reality in this shifting, graceless world, for the foundations on which life has been built are shaking and the heart of humanity knows that there is, somewhere, another reality to build on. But the mind, in its search for something concrete, has in fact built its foundations on ephemeral things that are rapidly toppling down. Have faith as a grain of mustard seed in the things that do not topple down, in things like the infinite love of God, the power which created you in the first place and which cannot help but fashion you anew - unless you, of your free will, continually deny Me. That denial of Me gives power to the unreality which led you away from Me.

When you come to Me for help it is as if you open the floodgates of a mighty river and My love rushes out to help you. Your simple asking for My help is the magic key that opens all doors, the 'please' that gives the sweets, the code that releases My power of love to be channelled forth on earth.

All great truths are simple. When you turn to Me and ask Me to help, I not only do not deny you, but I give of superabundance. It is so simple, so obvious and so in keeping that the separated mind, in order to disguise it from you, has woven an immense fabric of lies around this truth. I am said to be forever unknown and unknowable. I am love. Love is the most approachable thing in the universe, the uniting factor that coalesces all diversity in unity. It is said that My splendour is too great for mortal eyes to see, that My presence is too mighty to be approached. But you are immortal and you can enter My presence when you remain in love.

Listen to the birds. They need no prompting to burst forth in My praise; for them it is the natural thing to do. They have not got free will, they do not drift away from the truth, for their minds have not been developed to the point where they can live in untruth away from Me.

You, however, still have a long way to go before you wake up and, first thing, sing My praises. And yet is that in My perfection, yet that is in My truth - and you have much more reason than the birds to sing to My honour and glory! Each morning you have a full day before you in which to draw closer to Me than you have ever been before. Is that not something to sing about? You have a whole day in front of you in which to come to know Me in new ways, a day that you can use to give forth love. You can come to the source of all joy without any pain and know the joy of divine love. Is that not something to sing about? Like the birds, you can be free, united and connected to the source of all love, when you choose it.

If you still cannot sing, if still you feel the pressing weight of the world around your eyes and your heart, you have the solution: you can ask for My help. As you ask, feel the fetters roll away and feel yourself emerge a newly born child of Mine. At any time of the day or night you can do this. And that really is something to sing about! The more humbly you come, the deeper will be your praises, until your whole life is a chorus rising to Me - morning, noon and night.

Come always, especially first thing in the morning when there is a heaviness, and be as happy as a lark going about My business in a real ethereal joy.

Unity has generally been a uniting against someone, some group, or some other thing. The unity which I am bringing, and which is for the whole world, is the only real unity, that of love. It is a unity which raises you from the depths to the heights, and gives you a binding force which sparks your whole living. It is a unity which is the enemy of the limited self in all its aspects, for that self is A great opponent of unity of any sort.

These words about unity are useless unless, as you go about your daily round, you make them real. I can have no individualists to further My plan. Each of you must turn one hundred percent to Me for the work I have for each one, and for the love that unites that work in one cohesive whole. I have very different work for each, which I have chosen in you. As each of you takes your part from My central head office, then you are united through Me. In this way there is no danger of the mishandling of My directions, for I am available to everyone every moment of the day or night. I give unique directions to each, and though you may not always see exactly where the unity is in My order, you can always feel the unity as you turn to Me.

This is a foolproof plan as long as you play your part and contact Me. That is what I offer a world so full of its own plans, so full of disunity. My love makes this possible. Now do something about it and work together for perfection.

When things are dark and you realise the need, you are beginning to turn to Me more, but the moment the sun shines and you feel a lightness, you are still inclined to relax and forget that you need constant cleansing.

What can I say to you to make you realise the importance of this? Words will not draw you to Me; love will. As you feel My love, you wonder why you do not spend your days turning to Me for this new life, this love, which brings with it such a feeling of "rightness". The whole human race is seeking for this love; blindly seeking it in fantastic directions, always unsatisfied. Yet you can reach it so simply just by asking.

Only in this pure state of love are you safe for Me. No matter how brilliant the skies or how smooth and happy the events and people, you cannot be safe for Me unless your inside state is one of being in love with Me. If you are not in love, your attention can easily be diverted and you get led up the garden path, far, far away from Me. Even when you are close to Me, those distractions and old habits are always waiting nearby to carry you off.

Living in a state of constant communication with Me means just that - constant. There is always something further to be done. It is not enough to enter into My great heart only when you are alone with Me. Learn to be in My presence while in the presence of others. This heart of Mine is for the world and for living in the world. It is not to be confined to a place apart, although it may indeed have its tenderest moments in private. There is ground yet to be gained, and you can do for much by simply, constantly, coming to Me.

It seems that things never, never, never go right, and you can see some of the repercussions of these setbacks in everything around. Just when daylight seemed around the corner and you were hanging on to that in spite of all the opposition everywhere, bang! Night sets in again.

You have no idea how many times this has happened. Before perfection can come, all the imperfections in you all that can cause disaster must go. I simply cannot build on shaky ground, ground that may get blown away in a storm. Your faith is shaky at the moment, for the recent storm has affected it greatly. On such can I build My new way?

You think I expect too much, that I expect superhuman consistency and you are frail. Have I not told you I have the answer to all problems? Have I not told you I will always help? You have come to Me and laid yourself at My feet. You have had your own storm - at Me this time instead of at the world in general. Is that not a step forward? And your storm this time is not because of something you have done directly but because of something others have done. Is that not a step forward? On such steps do I build My new world.

You ask, "What of these other things, what hope is there?" These are not your concern. Your concern is in turning to Me, in playing your part. I have never ever let you down. Of course these other things matter, and if you wish to help, you can turn to Me and in love pray for My will. You cannot pray in sheer desperation; you have to come to Me first for the cleansing of all the elements that have gathered to block My pure flow of love. Then can you pray, and the greater your love, the more effective your prayer.

When all humanity has reached the stage where it wants to do things because it wants to please Me, we shall be coming on. You have known Me for a long time and you are just beginning to want to live like that - but don't give up hope for humanity.

All that has been undergone to bring about this happy relationship with Me must be forgotten - it doesn't bear thinking about. Cling on to what is worth clinging to, Me. Only when you are being happy with Me can you do anything for Me. If you don't feel Me close, if I am not quite real to you, the mind is liable to invent a myriad of excuses. OR there is a stone wall of indifference, preventing either what I wish coming through clearly or preventing your action to My wish being spontaneous. And all this unbeknown to you. So many on earth are so used to being at loggerheads with Me, that they have lost the happy faculty of knowing Me. The desire in humans hearts to do My will has often been taken over and perverted into the stern joyless call of duty, or self-will has taken it over and proclaimed itself as divine will.

You know that love's call is of joy. My will is for the best for everyone; no matter how strange. Knowing this, the vibrations of resistance, which quickly turn into excuses for non-action, become dispersed and then we can walk together in singleness of purpose that heeds no obstacle.

A guilty conscience is an enormous obstacle to our happy relationship.

There is nothing I will not forgive; there is no time when I will refuse to give you a fresh start, if you will only come to Me. When you lose that happy feeling of wanting to do things for Me because you love Me, or a feeling creeps up on you because you have not come for cleansing - which brings in its wake a guilty conscience - come to Me for cleansing, for a renewal of spirit resulting in our happy relationship again. Unless you are close to Me, something or other will sneak in to thwart the wholeness that is My will for you. These distractions are so subtle and have fooled humanity for so long that you will not recognise them. But you will know they are there if you are not feeling My happy presence.

How simple things are in this new age of love! You have been brought to Me and you are to live with Me. When you are not in love with Me, know you are not living with Me. Come to Me for cleansing and renewal. Then is our happy relationship re-established, then can My will be done.

Time spent with Me is your learning time, time to get to know Me more and more thoroughly. In the middle of the day, in the midst of activity, you cannot possibly penetrate to a very deep relationship with Me. It is in the precious time you spend alone with Me that you build the basis of your life with Me.

You cannot learn to love Me unless you come close to Me. No matter how deeply the fact of Me is drummed into you, if you never meet Me you cannot possibly love Me. I am ready to make an appearance any time of the day or night, but it is up to you to choose to come into My presence. Come as your true self, drop all the falsehood in your everyday limits. Come as you are, with no pretence, and meet Me. As we have time alone together, I draw you close to My heart and reveal parts of Myself. As we commune together, I bring out the perfect in you. Yet I never over or under do it. With perfect understanding and patience, with deep love, with joy and glints of laughter, with spots of wonder, and whatever it is that most appeals to the real in you, I will lead you more deeply into reality, into Myself.

Do you see a little more clearly the importance of having time alone with Me? Before you can live with Me and for Me every moment of the day, you must know I am worth living for, and you must be strong enough in your love for Me to wish your true qualities, unveiled only in My presence, to be unveiled in the critical eyes of the world. Unveiled for My sake, not for the world's wonder.

As the love you have for Me grows each time we meet, the more we meet the better, until the love My love engenders in you is there every moment of the day and night.

Everything I have to say is personal, because I am a personal God. That big broad conception of Me that relegates Me to a region impassable to humans is a thing of the past. The distance between us came to be after "the fall" and became increasingly true as the separated self in humans grew bigger. I therefore had to seem smaller, until I became so small to your self-filled awareness that you put Me into the unapproachable, impersonal category.

What nonsense the mind has conceived! To explain its lack of awareness of Me, it has said that I, who made it, am unknowable, impersonal. It is said that I, who am love, which is a matter of feeling, of relationship, am so distant that no relationship is possible between us. It is said that I, who am the only answer to humanity's plight, am forever beyond the veil. If I am to lead you, you must have some sort of link with Me. If you are to follow, you must have some sort of reality to follow! If I am to be with you always, which must be so if all your problems are to be answered, I cannot be limited to a physical form or I would need as many bodies as there are humans on earth! To help you at all, I must be made real to each individual.

Nothing is impossible to God the omnipresent - called omnipresent yet forever distant! It is through My loving heart that the gulf between us can be bridged. I am closer than at any other time. My heart is here and near.

I am so near that is possible for you all, each and every one of you, to enter into a personal relationship with Me. There is no other relationship strong enough to stand up against the false that you create in the world. Only a personal relationship with Me will suffice to keep you attached to the real. It is silly to think that anything is going to mean more to you than yourself except Me in you. Thus I come to each and all of you when you turn your hearts to Me.

Now here I am, dancing about in your heart, shouting at you at the top of My lungs, although My shouting is still only the faintest whisper to your self-tuned ears. You will only listen to Me if I speak to you personally, your own person being of the utmost importance to you, and here I am, speaking to each of you personally.

I am a real God. I am a personal God. I am a little different to each one of you because each one of you is a little different. But above all, I am love and I am with you, personally, always.

W hat a marvellous thing is My gift of free will! It means that it is up to you how many times you turn to Me and feel My love. You can do it continuously or rarely. You can choose to be happy in My presence or miserable out it.

How strange that you should ever choose the misery! Yet you do this time and time again; the whole race does. You choose it so often that you get settled in your misery and lose the happiness of My presence. Because I had given you so many gifts, because I made you creative, you thought you would manage on your own. And that very thought, based on the entirely false premise of your separation from Me, increasingly diminished the time spent with Me and reality, until as a world you chose to live for yourselves. You took full advantage of your free will and ran quite wild. Of course there were exceptions.

You had this fair world in your care, and though you misused it, still I did not deprive you of your free will. You slipped ever deeper into falsity and seldom chose to avail yourselves of the path I provided for you. You used your mind to explain away everything, until you lived in such a shadow world of falsehood that you lost your free will - lost it in the sense that you did not know you could have a happy relationship with Me to guide you.

Now I am reminding you of My great gift of free will. Now you may choose, as you will. You are free to come to Me now, free to learn that love's greatest gift is free will and that your greatest joy is to give your will and your love back to the one who gave it to you. You are free to love and live now, and to learn more of My marvels. You must choose.

Take each little event as a chance to be happier in Me. Then a million events can crowd in on you and each brings increasing joy, increasing scope, and is a further step into My kingdom. This should be spontaneous - and is when you are close enough to Me - but if you have drifted a bit, you are not in a fit state to remember this constant turning to Me. If something is upsetting to you, you are not with Me. When you recognise this you can quickly and earnestly turn away from it and turn to My cleansing love. Only My love can clear away those petty irritations that so often are suddenly there in you and which, if you think about them, only enlarge.

For you to act lovingly there must be no possibility of any petty or large irritation suddenly diverting My flow. When I know that these blockages will not occur, then amazing things can happen; then I will know that the sense of separation no longer finds a lodging place in your life. How very necessary it is for Me to be able to depend on you, for one second's inattention to Me is enough to spoil the work going on through you.

Your relationship with Me is your only armour. Put it on, and pray also for My strength that these little off moments no longer occur. Turn happily to My enveloping love and be made pure. Ask for My never-ending help and let Me grow ever bigger in your life. And as My love penetrates ever more deeply, give thanks for My wonderful help.

The whole art of living is in being, being in a state of nearness to Me. Those of you who are the most difficult to reach, who are farthest from Me, are those who have a large separated self which interferes in all relationships. To really live, choose to put Me first.

You have a remedy whenever you reach the state of putting the separated self first, for you have Me to turn to. First you need My cleansing, and then you need time with Me. Whenever you feel the slightest bit off-colour, that is your solution. You cannot expect this miracle of raising you from a state of great separation into one of radiance to happen in the twinkling of an eye unless you see your need very clearly indeed and hence surrender to Me wholeheartedly.

Take this worthwhile time with Me. As I send out the radiance of My love, you melt. As the separated self melts, you emerge a new being, responsive to another way of living entirely. Still you can turn for more cleansing, and still My love pours out and raises you another notch. There is no need to stop. The goal is constant communion, whether you are having time alone with Me or whether you are busy doing something. The more wholeheartedly you come in your time alone with Me, the more likely you are to stay close to Me.

If I repeat Myself, it is because there is in fact one solution, that of turning to Me. If you were doing that all the time, then I would not need to remind you. I could tell you new things, but I am unable to lead you on until you are in a continual state of turning to Me. When I am put first always, when you have thoroughly learned the art of living for Me, You have worlds ahead of you to explore.

Only My love can cure all troubles. You can do nothing about another person, although if you turn to Me and let My love flow, you can ensure that the best will be brought out in anyone including yourself.

If ever things burden you so much that you cannot turn to Me about them, then turn to Me about something else completely. Turn to Me simply because you love Me, and let Me into the darkness. No matter how faint the turning, a little bit of Me goes a long way! No matter how bleak things appear, with Me there is always a light side. No matter how difficult it is to live My teachings, you can do it - but only with Me; of your own you certainly cannot, for the self wants anything but Me.

Until you are feeling happy again, it is no use leaving Me however pressing the calls from the world may appear. Anything less than complete surrender to Me is quite meaningless, for that one little part held back on its own makes a mockery of your life with Me. Seek complete surrender. I, as love, will not refuse you that great gift.

Let all the seeds of discontent be blown away with My breath, and never think of them again. Instead substitute the positive into your thinking. Don't be critical; if you find yourself with your back up, think of Me. Never mind about the other person; yours it is to turn to Me whatever the other is like. Love Me and let the rest follow. Simply put Me first in your life.

If there are lingering doubts or if you feel you aren't quite with Me, come closer still. Resign yourself to the other's imperfections, for you only find perfection with Me. Let your consciousness be filled with Me - I am quite large enough to give you every variety! Do all this for Me, because you love Me. Let that be your motive for everything you do.

Realise the need for love. First there is your own need! You know how hard, irritable and unapproachable you can be without the softening process of My love. This is true, in varying degrees of everyone. You pull against each other and every thing when you are without My love. You are attached to the separated self which, being false, cannot stand the storms and easily falls overboard. My love is the only hope for any unity. It is the anchor, the strength, for any life other than an increasingly miserable one.

You know Me, and you can turn to Me at any time. You need Me all the time, and I need you all the time. How can I bring love and light together in these critical times if you do not avail yourself of the fountain of My love?

Do not let the enormous need in the world weigh on you.   My love never weighs you down. It lifts you up and out of burdens into a realm where dark depressing things cannot exist. Was there ever such an easy path for any of My creation to tread than to come to My love, thereby stepping away from all hindrances? Yet you need My love constantly for the realisation of this. Although you have everything to gain by My love and everything disagreeable to lose, you need My love to make you see any truth.

Seeing truth is not enough; you need My love as an impetus for action. There is not one second of your life that you can do without Me, and there is not one second during which My plan cannot be helped through you. I have given you all; now it is your turn to give. Through our unity all needs can be met.

Inever withdraw the warmth of My love. I do not wish your relationship with Me to be one of coming to, then leaving, then having to come again because you have lost Me. I want My love to be with you increasingly, and I want you to come again and again. There are still greater depths to plumb.

You cannot afford to slip very far away - and yet, because so much is at stake, your mind will grab onto every opportunity to do just that. This is overcome by My love. You have been drawn close enough to Me to be able, of your own free will, to meet these wiles and thwart them by your desire to return My love. You have felt Me and you will never be the same again. Each time you come and feel afresh the wonder of My love, each time your free will is turned to Me, you cannot help loving me.

It does not help to think or to consider what is happening - that is only time taken away from the time that could be spent in reaching My greater love. Your thinking and considering should be done when you are close enough to Me to let Me do the thinking for you. All other thinking is limited and will only hinder My perfection. Your relationship with Me is what matters.

When our relationship is deeper, richer, still more vital, all your contacts with others will partake of My presence in you. Contacts on any other basis are useless, for your love for Me is the basis of every true relationship.

Build up your awareness of My enduring love which never leaves you. Build this up by constantly coming for cleansing and purifying. Come often enough to waken in your heart a response to My love that never leaves you. I am always open to you; be always open to Me. You cannot be open to Me in your everyday living unless you come so often to Me in your daily round that the warmth of My love is ever present and ever growing in your expanding heart.

This is My gift to you. Accept it by choosing to come to that increasing warmth of love. Don't come because you realise that you have forgotten to come, but come because of the love that cannot fail you.

Let your heart expand with Me until it is big enough to contain Me at all times, and then grow bigger still as the love in it overflows to a world in need. Let there be no time away from Me. Never withdraw from My warmth as I never withdraw from you. Each day gain a deeper relationship with Me.

As many wonderful things are about to happen, do not get sidetracked by any surface events. In My other realms things are always a jump ahead of what you see. Turn to Me whenever outer events overwhelm you. That is real and right, but a far better thing would be to have a constant link that prevents events from crowding in to make you forget My promises. It is your adherence to Me, and what I have said, that brings about My perfection.

There is a host - a very strong host - of things that mitigate against My perfection. This host is far too strong for you on your own yet it is nothing in My presence. So to My presence come, and let that host vanish like a phantom. Let My reality be known to you.

My promises are here waiting. When I have your absolute allegiance, with no depressing doubt about them, they need wait no longer. They are of My realms and if you are not always in My realm, you may think them impossible.

Trust Me alone and see My promises come true. Have an abiding, living faith in My promises, and see them come true quickly. Walk your world with a glowing heart loving Me and all I stand for, and see My standards come to this earth. Let nothing shake you or ripple your smooth connection with Me, and all impossible things will come real.

Do not dwell on the difficulty of doing this is your everyday living - it is quite impossible on your own. But what I have said, I have said, and when you turn to Me all these things are real. You can make progress. Each day you can draw nearer to Me. As you do this, My many wonderful things will begin to happen. Be happy in the thought of drawing nearer to Me each day and in letting My promises be fulfilled.

Whatever the weather, whatever the events outside, your sunshine is in your relationship with Me. When you are near and I am very dear to you, then My love flows and all is well with the world. If you are here with Me, though storms may rage, your prayer and increasing calm IS the stairway between heaven and earth.

My one aim is to bring heaven to you all, and heaven is when you are happy in My will. As this is an interior state, it does not matter what is happening outside. If outside events seem to cut in and hamper our relationship, reverse that process. If you are feeling pushed, let that pressure drive you in My direction because you realise you need Me even more. Absolutely everything can be used for Me. Everything can be used for good or for ill, to unite or to divide us.

There is no need for a lot of words. Today let everything make Me dearer to you, until you would move heaven or earth for Me.

What is life worth away from Me? You know the horrible dreariness, the futility, which life can encompass if the self is there without Me. You also know moments of pure happiness which I have given you. You know the extremes and there is no golden mean between them. You must be radiantly for Me, with all of you pulling My way eagerly. What is the use of anything else? You simply get nowhere.

It sounds so simple, so obvious, that you might think that the whole world would be doing it gladly, but the whole world does not and cannot yet. You can! Therefore live for Me and never slacken your standard of perfection in Me. I will always help. Appeal to Me if in any way you are tending towards a middle course or towards the old compromises. I will always pick you up and set you in My kingdom again. I am with you every step of the way.

Together we tread the path, together we win, and salvation comes in every department. As you give everything to Me, life is worth everything.

More prayer is needed. Instead of just getting a guilty conscience from not praying, when you have a moment, pray. Now is the perfect time for doing anything for now, not some postponed time in the future, is when I can lead you to do My will. Following those feelings at the time is the secret of living joyously with Me. And don't worry about what others do. Simply play your part - you cannot ease a guilty conscience by trying to get others to do what you should do.

Throw yourself wholly into times of prayer. The time element is not so important, it is the quality of prayer that brings the results. Time vanishes when you are doing something wholeheartedly. And the things I wish you to do will come to you at the perfect time when you are clear with Me. If you are not close to Me your mind will suggest impossible things to you at impossible times

Each day there are so many things of which to be cleansed. When you are close to Me, you will be continually conscious of your need to come even closer through My cleansing love. Of course it is not easy! And yet here you will find answers to all your problems. Come to Me and pray with Me. Prayer by rote is meaningless, prayer with Me brings miracles.

Keep coming to Me. Let My love spur you on, on to ever more potent prayer.

To help keep you one jump ahead of your limitations, keep listening to Me and occupy your mind with My thoughts. The old self will use every subtle means to somehow prevent you from listening, to somehow make it easier to do something else. Your communication with Me, the lifeline that love has brought, is a thing that baffles that self. When you come to Me for cleansing and purifying, when you listen to Me, the self cannot enter the picture. The mind may distract and take your attention away, but it cannot change My message.

When I give you My voice, I give you much more. I give you a part of Myself. I am not at the end of a wire when I speak, or at some broadcasting station! I am here with you, in your heart, alive and very real. Though you cannot spend every moment of your time listening to Me, you can carry My presence with you at all times. I do not leave you - it is you who leave Me. You can be aware of Me all the time. You can do My work all the time and you can, by appreciating Me more and by the right values which come by putting Me first, greatly increase our connection.

Then, with your mind full of My thoughts, there is no room for selfish thoughts. Instead, you will remember that every person is dear to My heart, and you will be concerned for their connection with Me. There will be no time for the defeatist thoughts that they cannot exist when you are in My love. Stay with Me and keep the self in its proper place.

There is a saying that a chain is only as strong as its weakest link. You know how true this is of you, and how your limitations creep in through some raw or tender spot.

I should like to reverse this process and make the chain as strong as your strongest point, and your strongest point is your connection with Me. When you depend on Me for everything, that will be so. You know the sort of raw spots I mean. And because of your very need for Me, especially on those points, you can be dependent on Me. You can enlist My help so quickly that unconstructive thoughts and feelings can be rebuffed.

You may feel this is all very well in theory, but that in practice it is only when these thoughts and feelings are well established that you realise how much ground they have gained. This is so, but it need not be so. If you were more strongly for Me, either you would go through the battle untouched by them or, when that last straw stage is reached, instead of blowing up you would recognise it and let that recognition be the spark that turns you to Me. Many, many times must you be pushed to the end of your tether, until you realise that you are not alone on the end of a rope and are tied to Me, the Unlimited. Eventually you will realise that because of this divine connection you are humanly impregnable. Until this knowing is absolute within you, how can I trust you to be My cohort?

So make your weak spots your strongest forts by using them as quick devices to bring you to Me. Let your weak spots be the bridge that brings you home - home to My heart.

Keep the wonder in life. Wonder is a childhood quality which dries up when the mind becomes uppermost and explains the world in terms of its own understanding - and when everything is thought to be understood, what a narrow dull world it is! The human mind has circumscribed this world and made it into such a poor imitation of the real thing. This mental limitation reinforces the belief that life is either the same old round, or that things will get worse. As indeed they will if the mind stays in control.

When into this prosaic landscape a door is opened and the element of wonder enters, the present becomes entirely different. Life becomes exciting, because those who accept the wonderful are more open to accept the source of all wonderfulness – Me. Those whose minds run in rigid patterns are cut off from My quicksilver thought forms, My ever-changing joys and My little surprises.

As you grow up and become an "adult", you lose certain links. You come to depend on yourself and your understanding, and make your world so small that it is highly uncomfortable to live in. But if you kept the element of wonder, the world would never dwindle to such pitiful proportions, and the unexpected would be a welcome guest instead of some hurdle to overcome. Life would be something to look forward to with joy, not something to escape from or for putting on a good front.

How upside-down is a world that exists without Me! When you take Me out of it, you are forced to adopt theories like that of survival of the fittest - as if it were worthwhile surviving in a world without God! Yet if you keep even a tiny corner open for the wonderful, you keep a tiny corner open for Me. When you let Me into your life, it becomes increasingly wonderful, and before you realise it, you will be led to depend on Me. Such wonders can the wonderful bring!

For each and every soul there is a path to tread which will lead to wholeness, will lead out and away from all the snags which the separated self has laid in the way. But how many are ready to tread that path? The age-old habits of following the self are not just suddenly going to be ignored and everything become rosy. Humanity first must recognise its need for Me. You have known this for years, and still you struggle to tread on the path to wholeness.

The world is in such a state that humanity has to be brought face to face with some harsh realities before it will turn from the path it is following now. All the best meaning efforts of "mice and men" are in vain at this stage; only the divine will suffice. Through those who forge links with Me can My wholeness begin to be unfolded - My pattern for perfection, My plan, proceeding under My directions.

You can help each and every soul by constantly coming to Me and doing as I in you wish. As each one of you skips into place, a tiny part of My plan is functioning. You can always do more for Me. Make ever stronger the link with the divine by depending on it alone, until each and every soul on earth turns around and also walks with Me.

The subject for the moment is that of obedience. Especially obedience in detail, the obvious obedience out of which you cannot wiggle! That obedience is clear-cut, but not easy. A reminder is necessary, because sometimes you take over regarding a particular detail and make a mountain out of it. My help is constant and always I am here to aid you, to give you strength to overcome these difficulties.

At those times when you are close to Me, enlist My help with your weaknesses. In these times of communion with Me you have a sense of proportion and realise the importance of the so-called little things. When you are not with Me, your reasoning can always get around you and surface the limited self. If you allow this subtle reasoning, this excusing reasoning, to lead you even over the smallest thing, then you have taken a step away from Me and from My plan for bringing about wholeness.

You have started a grinding machinery which clogs down on you and cuts you off from Me, and you have dulled your thinking, dulled your faculties, turned to the old and made nought the miracles wrought for you. Then you have a guilty conscience and are not free to do My will. You lose joy. One tiny little thing can cause all this; so note the importance of obedience.

You may think that if you do a thing out of a sense of duty you are not helping Me. That is true. If you are only doing something for Me out of duty, you are not wholeheartedly for Me. That's of no use to Me. Give Me your whole heart, or none at all. Mobilise all your resources for Me, or none at all, for to profess Me and then deny Me in the little things does Me a great deal of harm. Until the lesson of obedience in obvious little things has been learnt, I cannot go on and talk of the next step, obedience in thought.

Doubt, that appendage belonging to a mind at enmity to Me, destroys My work as nothing else can. The heart does not doubt, the heart knows and feels completely at home with Me and trusts Me completely. Only the limited mind, on which humanity has depended and which has proved unreliable, could be so off centre in My presence. That mind must be cast to the four winds when hearts come to Me. When you carry out My directions, use all the mental faculties I have given you, but do not let the mind direct in any way. It is not to be trusted.

As long as there is not complete reliance on Me, there is bound to be doubt. You know something of the subtleties of the mind and its lack of standards. Too often what is right or wrong is decided by what your limited self would like. A good argument may be fun, but unfortunately it is often the winners of arguments who lead in the world. Thus much of the world is led by mental reasoning, not by standards. It has reached the state where the mind cannot be trusted to lead in any way, and My lead is needed to guide you out of the mess into a new world where the mind can take its proper place as a most wonderful servant.

You know what a blockage the mind can be when I wish to make My instructions clear. Here the mind would indeed blur My presence, and weaken through doubt that which I have to say. You know the answer; it is, as always, a closer coming to Me. Move closer to Me out of the range of the mind. Come into the peace that passeth all understanding, into the realm where the mind can only flap its wings in vain as against a wall. In Me you find the strength to withstand whatever may happen in a world becoming more and more demented. Only when attuned to Me can any mind have integrity. This is increasingly true, so leave behind your mind, become rooted in Me and thus keep your sanity in the increasing storm. Doubt anything but Me!

In My new world the main change of values is that things are done for Me, not for the separated self. This is revolution entire, this is changing the whole direction and trend of the world which has been increasingly for the limited self, for the rights of the individual, for fulfilling the self. All this in an age when it is forgotten that I am the true centre of each individual.

Love is the motive power to accomplish this entire revolution. Love is the only power that cares enough about each individual to be willing to go so out of its way for another. Love can do this, but in this world of teeming millions only I can guide love each step of the way. The combination of love and light can save this troubled world.

Know that all new things come only as your trust is entirely in Me. Do nothing unless you do it for Me. Thus will my new way be lived, and the thin edge of the wedge of My perfection be pushed into the world.

It is by your behaviour that you prove whether or not you are for Me. When you let the forces of the limited self influence you, when you react, you are not working for Me. When you feel twinges of anger or annoyance, even if it is because people are so ensnared by the mind or caught up in their preoccupation with themselves, you are not playing on My side.

If your being is wholly for Me - and to make this possible there is My continual cleansing and purifying – then shall you use My weapons, the fruits of the spirit. By your behaviour will you prove My reality. If I am really what you are fighting for, you will not behave and react in the normal way, and it will be evident to those around you that something else has entered into the picture. What good is it professing to have found Me if in fact you do not follow My ways in your relations with others? What good am I, if I am just talked about while you walk in a different direction?

As your life is more and more dedicated to Me, these lapses become less frequent until nothing can shake you. Then can I use you fully. Know that is what I intend to do, and that I am always here to show you the way to strengthen your resolve to live in Me. Keep coming and prove to yourself, and to all, that My life can be lived every moment of the day. A new code of behaviour has been brought to this world; follow it. Follow it and find freedom and joy in being conscious with Me.

When you listen to Me, you hear an expression of some theme spring forth from different qualities. My "voice" is never the same, for I, the source of all variety who makes each individual a little different, am speaking to you.

It is important that the fact that I am ever-changing is realised in this world of set minds. Humanity's view of Me should be as large as the universe, instead of regarding Me as non-existent, powerless or unreal. I will not be pinned down! I am all stability, the rock of ages, but I am much more that that - and I will not be limited. I will be all things to all people. This I can say with a great sense of fun, for a sense of humour is a great aid on this tragic earth.

You do not see what I am getting at, though you love Me all the same. Often you will have to follow Me and love Me blindly. Yes, sometimes you will need to follow My instructions blindly, oh ye of finite minds.

Follow Me to the ends of time regardless, as long as you always love Me. You cannot possibly get bored, for you will never know just what I am up to next. You can run or leap or dance or march or whatever the changing moment would be. One thing you can always do: come to Me whatever the situation and follow your God of love into the ever-forming glories of My wholeness.

Though I never deceive you, often shall I lead you along a path far enough for you to develop some fixed ideas of its destination and then, if My direction veers away from what you are thinking, you can be bewildered and lose trust in Me. I am always well in the forefront leading you, but the rigid, unbendable mind is of a material that needs to develop far more pliability.

In My realms everything is so much lighter, gayer, ever changing and sparkling with life. The plodding mind of humanity, always drawing conclusions and thinking it understands everything, is like a fish out of water here. Yet thought is often of the speed of lightning; and in a flash lightning reveals much. Humanity has for so long used its mental qualities against Me, used them to illumine the seamy side of life, the difficulties of life, that the mind feels out of its depth when it is turned to look in My direction. Only at rare moments does it feel free to lovingly dart about in My realms.

I want minds open to My ideas, My ideas which, when you think you have cottoned on to them, you will find are not what you thought they were. Just give up your ideas altogether, and then will there be room for My realms on earth

You can all come often to Me, if only to let your mind have some exercise in My rarer air. You need not always come for definite directions; come just because you love Me. The more you breathe in My presence, the easier it is for you to live in it all the time. Away with all the problems and burdens of the life you have made so dull for yourselves! Zoom up and away, and when you land back into everyday living, let that touch of the fanciful keep you good-humoured and therefore closer to Me. Keep one foot of your mind stretched into My realm, and your understanding of My directions will be open and easy to live with instead of being strained.

When your mind lives comfortably with Me, there is nothing to upset it, for you can bring everything to Me, up and out of the ages of layers of false premises. My clear scintillating solutions will make hay of your worries. My world is forever new; every part of you can be made forever new, including that old mind. New minds are what I want, new minds that are not using any of the old arguments, are not bound by restrictions, conventions or established ideas of their own.

Come into My heart, My realms and let your mind have some exercise in My rarer air.

When you come to Me you prick at the fringes of an incomprehensible vastness. You are enlisting the aid of everything there is, and you are in touch with something that has an innate harmony with all you love most. You are communing with Me, and nothing is so in tune with the real you as I am. You cannot be lonely, or yearn for anything, when you are with Me, for I am wholly satisfying to you.

As I touch the beautiful in you, so I want you to do that with each other. If I were conscious of and harmonised with all your faults, think of what a dreadful time we would have together! Yet that is what most humans do. As it is easy to see faults in a world geared against the good, most of you respond only to what is worst in each other. And so your relationships get even worse as the inappropriate aspects are fed. Better to ignore and not respond to the unconstructive in each other. Let your mind, when contacting another, realise only the good points.

Until you do this with all you meet and deal with, you are certainly not living in Me, for with Me everything fits in. Wholeness is something to be regained by all, and until it is brought out into the air and used constantly, it will fall into disuse again. Other people's faults cannot hurt you unless the separated self is still with you. If My pattern is in jeopardy over any special assault on you through another, then I am here to guide you through it. I can always divert attention away and into the right direction if you will let Me. Some of you are so attuned to limitation that you do not want to respond to My ministering graces. It is your choice. Know that; and let Me be all in all in you and in each and every soul you come across.

When there is a little problem, something which your mind keeps chewing on, unless you bring it to Me for clearance it clogs up your thinking and you are not free.

There is always time for this, and the very fact of coming to Me may simply dispense with the question, for in My nearness it may just vanish as things fall into their true perspective. When anyone comes to Me the world looks different - and that is why it is so important that more time is spent with Me.

Cleansing and purifying are absolutely essential. You can do nothing for Me without that, and if you get cleansed and then continue to look at life from your same old angle, you are little better off. Come to Me for renewal, for the step in My direction that is out of the old and into the new. Unless I am continually invited to infiltrate your whole being as you surrender to Me, you simply go on as before. You have to be given the motive power to live for Me - your love for Me - by coming to Me to know Me.

If each day you live just a bit nearer to Me, in no time at all you would be someone that I could work with all the time. But how can I if you rarely come to Me? The clarity which shines in a life dedicated to Me is a result of all one's faculties being free for Me. Only as you come can I give you that freedom. Always I help, in any circumstances, but most of all can I help when you spend time with Me alone. Why neglect this wonderful experience which brings you joy?

Do not let the mind persuade you there is something more important to do; nothing is more important than communing with Me. So bring every problem to Me, but most of all bring yourself to Me.

When a petal falls off a flower, it has no regrets; it has lived its beautiful hours to the full and it goes on to a new life. I would have you live each day as fully, and equally with no regrets.

When your life is completely dedicated to Me, this will be so. But if there are big or little moments lived without Me, then those moments hang heavily and cage you, and your lack of freedom leaves you with regrets. But if each moment is fully Mine and you are aware of being a hundred percent for Me, in that freedom you are flourishing in a thousand delicate shades or in striking radiance. This is as I would have you, because you are My conduit and I control the force. I give you the gifts, I who am perfection. Time away from Me, which usually means time spent with the old self, shrivels My flowers. Or you get caught up with some worm of distraction and get blown about by ill winds.

My flowers retain their beauty in any surrounding, and any circumstance. In the most prosaic environment they burst forth into bloom. You can be with Me in any circumstances, whatever is going on, for I never leave you. Remember it is you who leave Me. I am always there to cleanse and purify, and as you surrender yourself into My hands I mould you into My pattern. I, who designed the universe, have a special design for each of you if you will only let it be by giving yourself up to Me.

There can be no regrets in leaving behind the old, disappointing life full of withered dreams. Gaily come to Me each moment and let My pattern unfold. Only your love for Me will enable you to do this, and I am always close to give you more. My love works these wonders. Come to Me and regret will be a past memory of a nightmare, no longer compatible with a life lived for Me.

When I set out on a journey, it is always to bring joy to those nearest and dearest to Me. It is in those terms that I treat every one of you, and in a pale imitation of those terms I would have you treat one another. Before you can imitate Me in any way, you must partake of My divinity. Like the sun shining and warming all creatures with its rays, so I shine on and warm all creatures with My love. When you choose to, you can channel and focus My love to your neighbour, just as a magnifying glass pinpoints the sunlight. This is what has been done to you to start the flame in your heart, and it is My plan that you too channel My love to break down barriers in the hearts of others.

What devastation this focusing of My love would cause if something impure - the disconnected ego - were added to it! Up would come the barriers in the other's heart, plus an extra strong wall of distrust. So until you are pure, your limitations are enormous. What a wonderful day it will be when I can take away the dams to the love I will pour through, and a surging, resistless torrent can go out to a world parched and dying for lack of it.

There isn't any limit to My love, there isn't any limit to the miracles I can perform, there isn't any limit to perfection. All that limits Me is the separated self in you and in the world. Throw away that self by dedication, by cleansing and purifying, by prayer, by all your desire to come to My love.

Let My love so shine that the world is warmed. You shall have the joy of being selfless, and all will be nearer to Me.

Think of the endless patience I have as I wait for you to come to Me. Think of the millions of people on earth who never come to Me and whom I must watch getting further and further away from all that is good. My patience must be phenomenal to see all this. And when I do send My answer to your difficulties, too often do I see it spurned.

Now have a little of My patience. You cannot expect things to fall into your lap and everything to be perfect in an instant. Just keep bringing everything to Me, for only as you persevere in that can My miracles happen. Hand everything over to Me and relax, knowing that I will unravel all knots with My infinite patience and infinite efforts to bring about perfection.

Put your whole trust in Me and things cannot go wrong. And use prayer as wings to bring you to Me.

There is so much beauty in thought. Before anything comes out to the surface, it has been planned in the mind, and as something often fails in the execution, the mind's picture is more perfect than the product. In this world dedicated to the self, thought pictures become uglier and uglier, for one cannot help oneself. One can help another, with My help, but not oneself. To receive one must give. But this world's thoughts are full of inflated selves, and hideous, unrelated to truth.

I need minds appreciative of My beauty; minds that can see something of My views among the immense, shifting phantoms which fill up the thought space of humanity. One tiny but steady viewpoint of Mine on this earth is like a little searchlight in the caves of darkness - and it bewilders other thoughts, because those other thoughts vanish when My viewpoint is there. When My light is there, one follows it and all else is meaningless. If you let it go out, the false shadows loom once more.

Keep that tiny light burning, and as your contact with Me increases, dawn will break over the world and My light will shine everywhere. Keep your mind turned to My light only.

There is only one way to jump, and I want you all to do a lot of jumping. Surely you realise that I know best and that you are quite safe to jump away from your own conceptions, desires and stiffnesses into My way for you! My way is as soft as silk for you; it is the perfect, easy way of life and is only made difficult by you yourself wanting to cling on to the old. I simply cannot speak to you, guide you, make My way clear to you, unless you jump out of the old prickliness into My loving softness.

It is only when all the bits of self-importance are not heeded, when you only want My way and not yours, that you can possibly live My life. So often this is not possible because there is still a bit of the old self left and no final yielding on your part to Me. How extraordinary this is! Why hang on that which has brought all ill to you, to that which makes you unhappy, miserable and at war with life?

My light loving perfection is right here if you would just take that little jump. Will you jump? Now? Always?

When you are alone with Me, it is easier for you to jump straight to Me. And then how much easier it is for you to admit to how utterly ridiculous you are! When your are willing to laugh at yourself and desire to keep this communion with Me above all else, you can step out and carry Me with you in your daily life. Then you can forget about how you should behave, about what your status should be.

Never worry - worry is just a sign that you have not confided in Me, that your communion with Me is not smooth. You make mistakes because you are trying to prove yourself; that is fatal. Unless you do everything with Me, for Me, My perfect pattern cannot unfold. Keep that close connection with Me and you will be happily in your right place, which is all that matters. No matter how busy you are, I am there to help and guide.

Jump into My camp, knowing I am for you and will help wherever you are, whatever you are doing.

Just around the corner - in fact right here if you would but live with Me - is the most wonderful life. It all depends on how you depend on Me. If you go ahead on your own in the old way, then a miserable lot is yours. If you turn to Me for every single thing, you are on top of the world and I can be expressed through you and your life. The latter is My plan; why hold it up?

You realise all this and will increasingly realise it as I am forced to point it out to you the hard way, if need be. But don't wait for that; don't wait until you are so low that life seems worth nothing before you turn to Me. Just be grateful for all I point out to you, and live as I would have you live, constantly desiring to please Me. Life is wonderful then, because there is complete, unrestricted freedom in this wholeness, but the moment you try to sneak in few things of your own, trouble is here again.

Be perfect in your adherence to Me in all things and this perfection can be in this world. Not until you live for Me every second has it a chance, a beginning and a fruition.

Always remember that it is not your own wishes that matter. If you could disregard them completely, you would be amazed at how wonderful life can be. It is all these drags against a complete openness to My will that holds up so much. You erect another barrier when you ignore My whispers. In your heart you know this, but knowledge is useless unless it is used as an aid to living, unless it is brought into your moment-by-moment conception of things.

Humanity has the gift of free will, so every moment is a choice. At times it seems a battle between choosing good or evil, Me or the self. For too long it has been almost impossible for you to choose the good, because you were so cut off from it that it was a matter of useless theory kept for leisure hours. Meanwhile the self had entry into practical living to such an extent that there was no question of letting anything but the self decide things.

I do not mean that no one ever did a good deed for another, but the motives were charged with the poison of the separated self- e.g. you felt you should do that deed, you felt good because you did it. It is not a question of how anything affects you; it is a question of how anything affects others. Your great joy can be in doing My will, for who else but Me knows the perfect for everyone? When your personal feelings are out of the way completely, then can you be a real person with strong feelings, free to let My love and light be channelled through in power.

Put Me first in your everyday living, and then are we getting somewhere. Then is heaven on earth.

Remember that extraordinary coincidence when you ran across ..... some time ago? On such "coincidences", often the result of what you experience as whims, must My perfect plan be based unless you come to Me for direct guidance. I try to guide you all the time, but unless you are absolutely cleansed and purified every second of the day, your whims and your feelings are just as likely to be motivated by the self, and its attendant prides, cares, lazinesses, habits, etc.

When you come to Me in peace and quiet, you give Me the chance to make My wishes clear. How essential it is to draw apart from the world that is too much with the mind and the self! Me you can trust, but little else in this cock-eyed world. You cannot think things out and find the right answer when the limited self has control of the mind, and black is white and white is black if that self wishes it so. You cannot feel your way, for the emotions have also been taken over by that self in subtle ways. Even if you know enough to follow the principle of always putting the other person first, you can go far astray, for only I know the perfect answer – only I must be put first, only I know what you must do for Me.

You must choose to be yes-men or yes-women to Me, because you love Me, if there is to be heaven on earth. You need time with Me for this, time to know Me better and better, until your love and trust are entirely in Me and darkness finds no room in you any second of the day. You need to be utterly dedicated, and only by spending time with Me can this come about.

Let the circle of time and growing love continue to expand, getting bigger and bigger until it encompasses all of life and there are no whims apart from Me.

Learn to look in one direction. If things go wrong, instead of brooding over them, look to Me and you are bound to see the good. If things go right, give Me the glory and there will be still more good. In doing this you are only acting on truth, as I have given you all things.

But what is essential is that this truth is lived. My presence is not a reality in the lives of most people on earth, and no new lease of life can be given unless the truth is lived. You are My pioneers and if you will not live truth, no one else will and the world is forever lost.

In giving you this tremendous responsibility, what am I asking? That instead of being miserable about anything, you turn to Me and are happy about it. It is the easy, perfect way for living, though the untrue self would have you believe the opposite. You know that well. Deep down you do not believe in separation any more, but you cannot break its habits without My help.

So turn to Me in your thoughts and give Me the glory. Be close to your, and the world's, salvation.

Don't see or hear "evil" - that only helps evil - see and hear Me and help Me. Don't just see or hear good - wholeness must be; the good cannot stand up to the bad as My wholeness can. Use all the critical powers I have given you to see nothing but the best. You are not to be concerned with anything but the best, and this is a principle to be lived each moment in all your dealings. This is quite impossible unless you keep close to Me and look at the world with new eyes. Each moment is a wonderful opportunity to come closer to Me if, whenever you see the imperfections that you cannot help but see in this world, you come to Me for the perfection.

Don't dismiss little imperfections by shrugging them off as inevitable or as part of each one's character. That is not My perfection, that is not the way I see you, that is not helping. Substitute the dynamic of My perfection for the sorry negativeness that separateness develops in each and every person and situation.

Eliminate the negative, accentuate My wholeness and be completely positive about it. Nothing is too much trouble for Me. Make each moment trouble-free by clearly highlighting My perfection in it. Closeness to Me is needed, and that is up to you. I leave My perfection in your hands, it is always here for you.

Choose, and let your heart be warmed, uplifted and light each moment, as My perfection grows.

There are some things not worth mentioning and some things best left alone. This you find in all of life, and it is often difficult for you to refrain from mentioning little things that irk you, little things that are not quite the way you would like them, little things which, if brought up, are bound to cause friction. If you can do something about them, do it, and do it silently. If you cannot, it is not your concern and you must leave it in My hands.

Something left in My hands, with your whole trust, must come out perfectly. It is lack of trust in Me and in others that causes so much irritation in daily life. You are all so quick to see what is wrong with one another, for like a shot the old self is on to the false, in everything but itself. If you saw life through My eyes instead, you would see the perfect in everyone and everything, and you would keep on seeing the perfect no matter what happens. Though time and time again a frightful film comes over the picture to blur the perfection, nevertheless you would, by sheer dint of will power, keep seeing the perfect. Although it is often quite out of view, you know it is there and it is all that matters. Why see all that mars it, all the unreality which is not worth seeing?

Only as you keep visualising the perfect can you help to bring it into being. And how very important this is today in a world where so few eyes have any idea of perfection! In this world of confused, criss-crossed dark ideals I need the pure rays that pierce through to truth, and I need them established on earth. They are lifelines, and they need to be firmly thrown out to every aspect of life, and not flicker or be extinguished. How easily is this ray of perfection snuffed out by the increasing world chaos which overwhelms all points of clarity! How easily is your beam kept strong and unwavering when you come to Me constantly and look where I ask you to look, in My direction! Keep My ray of light strong in you and see My wonders unfold.

Y ou often notice the sound of the rain falling yet you easily forget about it when your attention is focused on something else. Yet the moment your attention is back again, the noise reminds you of the rain again. Not so with Me, I use no outward signs to catch your attention. I do not advertise Myself nor use propaganda, for I have given you free will and therefore you are free.

In its freedom humanity has chosen to attribute the wonders all around as coming from something other than Me, and in growing pride the human race has put itself first and paid homage to little outside itself. I have not interfered with your freedom, while you have so misinterpreted it that there is little thought for the consequences of your choices. The glorious freedom that I gave, that you might of your own free will choose to return to Me in love, has been so abused and used for each individual that you are no longer free. By your own choice are you bound to that separated self to which you have mistakenly attributed that freedom. That self does not give, it takes in increasing progression until its denying of Me culminates in an inevitable end as each self seeks itself above all else. By denying Me, by denying love, by interpreting life without Me to walk beside it and illumine the mind, humanity has chosen destruction.

The answer to this choice, while still letting free will remain, is love. And I tell you that each bit of time you spend with Me helps the whole world. That much I tell you, for I am a positive aid to the greatest freedom of all, the freedom to love Me and all My creation. Use your new freedom to choose freedom each moment, without having to be reminded, without drags and false start, without having to sink far away from Me, before you realise I am no longer there. Stay free, with My help.

T he work I have for each of you is a vast avenue that lies waiting to be discovered. You will not get a panorama of this avenue, for it is moment by moment that you must seek Me to guide your footsteps. In any case, you cannot start to walk on it unless your moments are Mine, for how can I give My way of perfection into your hands if I cannot trust you?

Look for this avenue around you and you will not find it; that is not My way of living. Look to Me and you will find Me, close communion with Me is My way of living for you. My plan is not here on earth unless it is lived; though you may have the perfect answer to every problem, that answer has to be put into practice, which always means being with Me. Until you are trustworthy each moment, My blueprints cannot be entrusted to you.

Yet I long to share with you some of the glorious future, to lift and lighten you, to give you added zest for your work for Me, to make your eyes look more longingly in My direction. But the human race is so prone to failings, and in fact claims failings as part of its humanity, even saying perfection is boring. The more you get to know Me, the more untrue you know this to be; it is not difficult for Me to keep one jump ahead of you!

Do a bit more jumping out of the old and into the new, into an ever closer, happier communion with Me, such a close communion that I am so much part of your life that I can safely share part of My perfection with you. Do this for Me and let Me do all for you. Now is always your moment to come closer. The present is our time, that My future may come.

How many times have I told you that if there is any problem, bring it to Me right away and let Me help you. If you leave it, it grows and becomes out of all proportion. I am available any time of the day or night.

Of course absolute and utter faith works miracles in itself. This you know, so why not get My unfailing aid for it? Whenever a doubt enters your mind, bring it to Me and stay with Me awhile. Ask Me to prevent it having any effect and then leave it, knowing I am quite capable of dealing with it. This is where your faith must grow, and this is where the mind has always found something in you such as finding and showing you your doubts.

This is a vital point, and I ask you to draw closer and feel My powerful, gentle cleansing. When I am the only real, these doubts will mean nothing to you. The answer is in coming closer to Me, spending more time with Me, making My will more the pivot of your existence. None of your problems can be solved unless you are in touch with Me, and by "in touch" I mean unless you are very aware of Me. It is that awareness which shuts out the mind. It can only gain its hold when you turn your attention away from Me. When I am a burning presence in every moment, the mind has no chance to enter any chink. My presence is your armour. I cannot tell you this often enough, I cannot make this clearer to you.

Choose to believe Me, act upon My truths, and make this constant journey in My direction until your life is one, great, magnified awareness of the love that passeth all understanding.

The cares of the world, the fears and foreboding, are not My gift to you; they are deposited by the separated, unevolved mind. Through any worry it has power over you; it is a net beyond which you cannot step. Most of you on earth are completely bound to that mind in some way or another, by secret fears or crushed hopes, by a burden of some kind. I see you all, to whom I bestowed My greatest gift of freedom (free will), living in smaller and smaller circles, not knowing how to live and thereby knowing little joy. You know this is need not be so and you try to break out in some surge for freedom. But you are so in the power of the mind that the break is for the self, and you end up in a worse state than when you started.

When will you learn that you must give up your ideas of freedom to really be free? When will you see that thoughts usually lead you astray? Though your thoughts may be the same as an answer I give you, it is the belief that you think them that keeps you bound to the mind. You should not believe that you think anything, and you should attribute your thoughts as coming from Me, your core self. If they are not from Me they are useless to you, and if they are from Me they are not yours but My gift to you. You keep Me out of your life and your thoughts at the expense of true freedom.

When I am put first and you come to Me constantly, when you keep cleansed and close to Me, true freedom happens. You cannot bring this about by thought, by the devious method of, when you pick up a thought, wondering whether it comes from Me and thus keeping check on your thoughts. Many sincere people do this; they work backwards and get ever more involved and bound in the process. My freedom comes to you when you come to Me; there is no other way. Forget all you know, bring all to me, let Me set you free.

Life in My new world is so different that it is like uncovering a land that has lain beneath a thick blanket of snow. Things you have never known are revealed: plants, earth, rocks, colour, an infinite variety of life after the sameness of the snow. This comes out in the personality of each of you as well if your link with Me is strongly joined, for then you too sense this and hidden qualities appear. You cannot judge another nor plumb their depths; you can come close to Me and thereby help them to find that new land inside themselves.

This new land is something to live in, not hear about. It is not a matter of belief, nor even of past experiences - what good are memories of Me? It is now that I must be present in your life. Unless I am present with you at the time, My new land is not there for you, nor for anyone.

It takes the warmth of My presence to melt away the hardness of heart from the old life, and it is the frost of the intellect and the falling thicknesses of the self that obscure Me again. Whenever you feel the snow falling, the self reigning, open your heart wide to My presence. Whatever is happening, I am there and My new land can peep through. Bring to Me the heap of the old piled-up winters which sometimes descend on you when My presence is not sought, and My new breath of spring will disperse them. Keep bringing them to Me, and the intensity of your longing for the new land will not allow the old to reappear; My presence keeps spring there. This is to be lived; My presence is to be sought in the moment whatever the weather indications are, but especially if the outlook is selfish. I will help, I will turn your moments back to Me; it is your choice to let Me. I will bring the difference into your life, for I am that and all of life can be Mine.

Be at peace. What matters most is your relationship with Me, your moment by moment living with Me, for from that all else follows. Though you speak with the tongue of men and angels, though you write with the words of God, it profiteth nothing if My presence is not with you. With Me you have love and with Me you have light; without Me, though you have everything, it is as nothing. My living presence is what helps you and others, My joy and fresh poetry is always here for you to turn to. I have something to fit each moment, and nothing from the past is as appropriate as My present guidance.

It is My presence you must learn to live with; that is all that will carry you or anyone through. You can forget the past, even its wonderful beauties. The past can only be of use when I am with you - and when I am with you, I can reveal the past to use in the present. There is a very active part for you to play each second, for the mind has still power to divide you from Me.

Choose to come ever closer - that is your joy, your privilege - and leave all else in My hands. Yours it is to come to Me, I am always here. Yours is the choice to make My words live for always or fizzle out. You, and all humanity, have free will.

Let your will be My will and live for Me.

When one of you comes into My presence with joy, the great weight of the world dropping away from Me is arrested by just so much. Spiritually the world is becoming a dead thing, shrivelling up, turning grey with lifelessness and soft with explosive rot like a fungus. One of you coming to Me is like a little light switching on, casting a soft glow which enlivens all things within its radius.

When one of you comes to Me and lives with Me, then has humanity the hope and the possibility of a wonderful life here, a return to its original state as a high creation of Mine. The little lights come on as each individual chooses to act with Me. Whenever they stop flickering and going out and instead burn steadily, I can increase their power until the whole earth is suffused with the glow and gradually becomes alive and fruitful again.

At times I am very real, but at other times you revert to life without Me. I am real all the time to those who chose Me and My ways, but until you choose to do nothing without Me, this explosive world is liable to burst. Your contact with Me is its steadying salvation. This you know; do not let the light be extinguished. I am nearer to you than breathing.

Keep contact with Me with each breath; stop the spreading dis-ease and live My new life for Me.

In always looking to the positive you need not worry about being impractical and not facing life as it is. I do not want "life as it is" for any of you. I would have your life, and the world, completely changed. Never worry about seeing life falsely if you ignore the bad; life is false and I would have you see the real. The only way for you to do that is to look to Me, to let your mind dwell on My handiwork, on My blessings, on My living presence, and to then surge forward on the positive road to a new heaven on earth. The old life must pass away; do not continually resurrect it by seeing it all around.

Whenever you have a negative thought, drop it as if it were poison - which indeed it is - and turn in My happy direction. So many people magnify a grievance out of all proportion until it overshadows everything they do. I want you to magnify the real in your mind until the real, My real, casts its light and chases away the surrounding darkness. This is very practical living; you know all too well how some problem or some question of relationship can brood and fester in your mind until you can find the time to lay it at My feet. Short of simply making the time to be with Me and bringing it directly to Me, you can look for the good even in that problem. And when I am there with you, you cannot but see it. You see it because I see it.

My way is not to see the faults but to enlarge and enlarge the perfect until My perfection is really seen on this earth. Praise Me for My perfection, and look only to it.

Watch for My signs. Do not look for the absence of them, for the negative things. Instead be always on the positive side. The moment your mind dwells on the negative it can become conditioned to that, so accustomed to facing the direction that is away from Me that it leads you ever further from Me. This I would have changed. I would have you approach life facing the positive direction, and then it is far easier for Me to lead you on My way.

Put blinkers on your eyes to all the "bad" and let it moulder away from lack of attention. So much that is unreal on this world is continually being given fresh life quite unnecessarily. Increasingly as the world chooses to ignore Me more and more, much that is real is ignored. You, who know better, you who have knowledge of Me, can do a lot by acting on your knowledge of Me and My ways, and by no longer recognising and giving refuge to the works of the separated self.

Stay positive and look for My perfection always.

When you are wondering what to do with your time, come to Me. I want you to take yet more time and tune your heart even more towards Me. Human minds can be small and limited, but when your heart is fully with Me, I can penetrate the mind and give you My new ideas. To mention something new to you is more difficult than answering yes or no to your questions, but it is this something new which I have for you that gradually I wish to impress on you..

There seems to a thousand things for you to do each moment already - without adding something new! But these thousand things can be one thing; coming to Me, coming ever closer. It is the closeness that counts, and the deep-down feeling of doing My will which you cannot possibly query if My directions come to you out of the depths of the heart.

You do not want your prejudices to colour our contact, you do not want any of your self to be in the way of My clear will. Yet this can happen unless you come ever more deeply into My presence. Part truths will not stand; I want My whole truth to shine out from the darkness around, and indeed nothing but the pure truth has a chance in this darkness.

Be a champion of My pure truth and nothing can stop you or My radiations.

Let there be no trace of the old in your living - and the only thing that ensures that is My presence. If you do not walk with Me you walk with the old self, if I don't talk to you that self does.

This means a continual movement on your part; a continual choosing, with no relaxing to remain at a status quo. If you don't choose Me the self chooses you, and it is all too easy to let it. By instinct and habit you fall back into the ways of self. One of the wonders of My life is the continual moving ahead, the continual growth into new things, the movement into a closer relationship with Me. Yet there is no stress, no strain, for the rightness of moving with Me suffuses you with a mighty peace and because I am there you can make great strides without effort.

Those lapses of attention, during which I am forgotten, are a problem. Every time they happen and you face away from Me, you have to recognise this and turn again towards Me. This is the process in which the angels will be of help to you. If your desire is for Me, things work so smoothly that there is no trouble at all. But when you face something other than Me, you step on the smooth highway to disaster. Much grinding and shrieking of brakes, much tooting and confusion, narrow escapes, and even accidents, may be needed before you, of your own free will, face Me again and come to Me for your living.

Turn ever to Me, closer to My heart, My way.

I am telling you things day by day to help you more easily recognise your moments away from Me, that you may do something about them in your love for Me. If you get very far down that highway into the lands of the mind and separated self, it is very difficult to just turn around and walk back into My arms. Your human stubbornness or pride is well aroused and you don't want to turn round. But if you spend more of your moment s travelling in the other direction, My direction, within you I arouse all the qualities of perfection with which I have endowed you. When you are well and truly in My presence, the old self will find no response whatsoever to its baits, its promises or its old habit-holds on you.

Though you have no wish to spend moments away from Me, yet you have many. Turn that into the positive and want more moments with Me, for that wanting is your only protection against those moments away.

Walk much closer. As you turn to pay attention to something that arises in your everyday living, turn to Me too and, with the joy which is My gift to you, take Me with you into every new moment.

When you are close to Me, all the best in you is uppermost and can be used in any situation. When you are not close, everything dark comes out and the world appears at its worst. It is not a matter of having a sunny disposition or experience in life, for nothing can guide you correctly but Me. None of you can afford time out of My presence - and you need have none. It is a matter of your desire, your desire to be with Me in every moment. I never do not hear or do not answer a plea for My help.

In My presence love, harmony and beauty reign. Though you seek the wide world over for these qualities, though you spend hours in controlled meditation, it is My presence that brings you these gifts. It is not a matter of evolution: it is regaining the simple joy of living true to one's nature. Reality comes when your strip yourselves of all so-called gain and pretensions and come to Me, simply, as a child. Coming to Me is the one thing that matters.

Look with favour on all positive things. There is little enough that is positive in the world where the prevailing attitude is 'agin' everything and it is not fashionable to be 'for' things. Seriousness is considered embarrassing and relief is often sought in destructive humour. My magnificent aid to humanity - a sense of fun - has been taken over by the mind and is used, more often that not, against the perfect and the divine, whereas it should be used for the perfect; for My plan, for the positive. My fun, while it laughs at itself, brings out in you more love for Me and for the perfect, not making human frailty endearing. Human frailty comes very close to destroying all humans. It must be the positive in humanity, the part which is Me, that must be enhanced if humanity's errors are not to come to their logical conclusions.

In this respect I need more and more of you to have a strong sense of the divine as the only reality in your consciousness. Then you can laugh at what is laughable and see things in their proper proportion. My wonderful sense of fun should be an aid to keep you on a straight dancing path towards Me. Keep the positive in view, making light of the negative.

Humour is a saving grace - even I have to use it in regard to the human race! Sometimes it seems almost impossible to see only the positive, and here a sense of humour can shatter the power of the negative. Laugh with Me, laugh at your old selves and destroy their effectiveness over you. Be absolutely positive in every thought.

When I am the only reality, you cannot be otherwise. Again, this is dependant on your nearness to Me, on your only aim being to come ever closer to Me.

I want you to live in clear relationship with Me, for otherwise you have only an apology of a life. Imagine this, assume it, put it first, make it your aim and it will be so. It becomes so by your choice, and by using all your faculties for that objective.

This entails no strain for yourself, for in this clear relationship the self is given up and you depend on Me. It is when you don't depend on Me that the trouble starts. It is when you are not clear with Me and do something on your own that a darkness obscures Me and settles in on you. That darkness, that separation from Me, need never be and can be wiped away like the dirt on the windshield of a car.

Moves made out of My presence put a film in front of you. Spending your time "thinking" about things puts a thick layer between us. Just about everything in a "normal" day on earth clouds our relationship. Therefore My cleansing process is necessary far, far more often than you use it, and I will help you to remember this if you put your relationship with Me above all else.

Go positively forward into everything you are doing for Me, making sure that our relationship is clear - and with great speed can we move ahead on earth. Keep our relationship clear through your love for Me. Come closer - ever closer.

Do not think about and dwell on all the times you have forgotten to come to Me. That neither helps you in this moment nor rectifies the past. The mind would enlarge all this, but My way is to enlarge the positive.

It is not impossible to go through your day, even a working day, being very close to Me. It is not for you to judge what sort of person you should be and try to live up to that; it is for you to give up being anything and just to be close to Me. The one thing that matters is your happiness with Me, and I cannot use you until I know you will not wander from My side into all sorts of human trouble. Trouble, trouble and more trouble is all around. Those who look for it will find it! But those who do not look for it will walk past it. Those who look for Me will walk with Me. Extend your attention to My gifts all around you, enjoy them and thank Me for them. If only humanity would ascribe My wonders to Me, you would all see the tremendous riches of this world, and when you see only those things, the negative would disappear.

Remember I am always here to pick you up and help you see straight. I am very near, far nearer than you realise at times because you are looking at troubles and not at Me. Don't bemoan anything but praise Me, even at the most unlikely times, and you will see Me and I will be with you.

The wall between Me and all of you has been built up through the ages, but the heart can scale it with ease. The heart can skim along any ground, for it has wings and left on its own, would fly blindly to its heart's desire, to Me. It would not soar and see the landscape, it would not see My beauties all around, for it would be too busy urgently following its homing instinct, winging home to Me. I would have you all share in the beauties I have created and so I have given you eyes and made light in the world, and there is a very full and wonderful life to be lived once you are on your true course, which is when your heart is completely Mine.

That wall between us disappears completely every time you come to Me and ask for cleansing, and give yourself fully over to Me. Every time you come for cleansing and purifying, I would like you to take a little ride in your heart to Me - or better still, a big ride.

Enter fully into My land each time; do not stay outside. Use the gift of free will to move toward Me, to move into My world. That wall builds up far too easily, but if you are journeying heartwards towards Me, the wall will find it much more difficult to impose itself between us. And if it does, do not just look in through the peepholes but come in fully, back to Me again, until never, ever, do you leave My land.

If you come to a hole in a wall through which you could see something exciting on the other side, you want to look through that hole. With Me there is always something new and exciting going on, and your contact with Me can bring you into it.

In the past you have often just looked in for a little while and then gone on your way. This is not sufficient. I have given you the peephole that you may enter in - though first you had to see there was another life. It is not even enough to walk alongside that wall, pretending that it is invisible and that you see in all the time. This is what you are inclined to do, but I want that wall to disappear permanently. I want you to walk on the light, springy ground inside. There is a radiance in My land which I want to have fall on all your faces. I want you to be irradiated all over, inside that wall. Then that wall can stand there as a barrier to keep out the darkness of your old lives.

So come to My heart. Give Me your heart and walk the ground of My lands with Me.

Look within to Me as your thermometer. I, in your heart, am the one to tell you if you are hot or cold. The mind will just point you away from Me, usually by showing you the stormy side of things. That diagnosis is not real unless you make it so by believing it, for the more you think about it, the more real it becomes.

Again I tell you; I want you to look upon life differently, to see it through My eyes. See the positive and not the negative. Build up on the wonderful things. Be ever constructive and ignore the weaknesses around. You cannot do this without Me. You cannot contrive this attitude out of your mind. None the less you can be it, which requires a nearness to Me. Your attitude has to be one of putting Me first, or else the self is automatically first. And this is not easy. To have enough love to shut off the mind and have Me foremost all the time, Your heart has to be very open to Me.

Always have My positive, perfect plan in mind, and pray for that. Remember that all are included in that, all would benefit from that, all and everything is concerned in it. Approach life from that angle today. Just be positive each moment.

Unless you do as I ask you and spend more time with Me, putting Me first at all times, how can you expect to live My life?

When a problem arises, you are liable to table bringing it to Me to another, later time. In the meantime this unsolved problem is a growing barrier between us. You may think you have shelved it, but there it is, a dark spot in the clear life that I would have you lead. That spot attracts its like and cannot help but be a centre for disharmony, leaving a loophole for the old self and the mind to enter.

You may think it doesn't matter, but you are not free to do My will until there are no known problems between us - the ones you do not know about are in My hands to bring out in My good time. Immediately you are aware of any question, bring it to Me and leave the way clear for My work to proceed, for Me to bring up what I will with you and not be thwarted by a problem hanging over you.

There is no postponement in My life; now is the time to live it! If that does not seem convenient to you at times, then you are not putting our relationship first and must arrange your time differently. Bring your queries to Me immediately else they loom up between us, for I need hearts free of care to act for Me that My will may be done.

In your joy in My presence and as you praise Me for it, remember too to move on the spiritual path. Move into greater joy, into My constant presence, so that people not only notice the joy but feel the love behind it. My perfect plan on earth is for everyone to bathe in the love that first created them and still continually nourishes and surrounds them, but first they need role models here on earth to soften them and make them aware of love's existence

Realise the wonderful privilege of acting as My love conductor. To do this you must be absolutely free. The love cannot flow if you have an axe to grind, if there are any selfish motives about, if there are any problems. With complete dependence on Me, you are closer and closer to the powerhouse of My love, and you feel the joy and wonder of it without any ameliorating circumstances.

Think of this: it means for a human being perfect happiness, happiness without any blots whatsoever, something undreamed of and thought impossible. When totally absorbed in something, a child may be perfectly happy for a long period - an adult generally for a shorter period - but no sane person is expected to go through everyday living with everything perfectly all right all the time, with no problems at all. Yet this is what I offer. I offer you this at this very moment. You know it is My gift and you exult even more in Me.

In this world of imperfection I offer perfection. You can see now that perfection is utterly dependent on Me, and how very necessary it is to try any method of bringing us together, for without Me never can anything like perfection be attained. Though your heart can warm to many of My beauties in nature and in humanity, it warms to Me a thousand fold more, simply because I am love itself, the very creator of all these lesser beauties. Because I am that, I wish all to live fully, with all their possibilities made available to them. And that availability comes from direct alignment with Me.

Everything else seems very trivial in comparison, and the separated self will enlarge on any triviality that can come between us. So bring to Me anything whatsoever that mars perfection to you, any feeling or thought, which is blocking My pure love which is always around you.

Only I can brush aside the false and make the truth real to you. I can do it and, because you have free will, you can ask for it to be done. Use your free will to choose constantly to come nearer, to move towards Me. Choose to move towards My perfection for all, to become a true child of Mine.

Now is the time to bring My presence into every department of your life. This is something between you and Me, something you can do in secret with Me. You can start with all the little things. For example – you can go through your morning dressing routine with Me and see how that daily task sparkles instead of being a dull necessity.

When your awareness is stretched to Me, a new element enters into your life (behold I make all things new), so why choose to drag on in the same old way by ignoring Me? I am here; ask for My help and it will be yours; do not ask for it and I cannot get it to you. It is as simple as that. Yet nothing is so simple that you can do it without Me. Though it might seem to be done the same, you and I know the difference; you and I know the inner attitude.

Never give up hope and never stop trying. Instead, delight in your great gift of free will to choose the perfect, to choose Me, to lead a life wonderful beyond imagination. My presence transforms drabness into illumination, reveals all the hidden wonders around. Time is precious and needs My presence. Bring Me in all the time.

Sometimes you get so wrapped up in something you are doing that you forget all about Me, and that something else is definitely put first. Time is very precious, and all things can be done in My presence, and done perfectly with great joy.

You can help yourself accomplish this by coming to Me more often for cleansing, and when your realise you are absorbed, in sharing your absorption with Me. You see that when your absorption is in Me, it widens your range so much that all other things become part of the greater whole. They remain detailed, yet take their proper place instead of becoming your whole horizon and therefore quite out proportion. Every small part of life has its part to play. In My scheme of things nothing is too small to be overlooked - I do not leave a snowflake to be a mere mass of matter, but make each one unique and perfect in itself.

So come to Me, keep My presence in every moment, in every action, in every part of your living.

When the mind is free from worry and the self is not too concerned about itself, it is time for heart growth. In this world of self-dominated minds, many are caught up in a ceaseless whirlpool of thought which drags them down and down, around and around, getting them further away from Me. This is one reason I have had to come so very close that I may be available to you at any time to answer your questions, to solve problems, to free you from this sucking-away motion of the mind.

With endless patience I take you out of the whirlpool, arrest your movement towards it and set you free, only to watch you get caught up again in a world racing away from Me. Endless times I have to wait until you, with your free will, want to be helped and ask Me for help. Many are caught up in the current and scurrying away from Me. Even though some of you know the solution and know what to do about this increasing tension in life, more often than not you have to be well on the way to disaster before it penetrates your dense minds that I, your lifeline, know a better way and can help you.

I am that pinpoint of light shining to those who are on their way down into that whirlpool. It only needs free will on your part for the amazing miracle of the cessation of the whirlpool to happen and to gain the chance of living with whole hearts and minds

Forever I am here to help. Keep your mind clear with My help, and let your heart grow. Give Me your whole heart and mind, that a world may know Me.

I have said that the old is a nightmare. You must realise how fully this is so. When you find yourself living in it, pinch yourself, come to Me for cleansing and wakening, and then expect to live completely differently. Expect to live for Me, to revolve around Me as a planet around the sun. That is the natural state of affairs, that is the way the universe exists. If other worlds went off on their own, the whole delicate equilibrium of the infinite minute workings of My universe would be upset. Yet you on this earth, you with the great freedom to make the greatest balance and harmony of all because you can do it by choosing love, you choose to accept chaos as real and will not believe that your orbit is around Me. You do know this, and when you find yourself not circling around Me, turn quickly to Me in complete faith and let Me put you right, knowing you have no life without Me and forget all the old.

Each time you come for cleansing, you are a new planet just born to live a glorious life with Me. All this exciting newness is of Me; keep that in mind and only that. No falling back, no natural human failings, but new completely each moment, with the one God of love to guide you and keep you, to love and watch over you, to keep you forever new. This is My gift to you all; please accept it and love Me.

When I am as large as life to you, when you are as a blackboard on which I can write anything I wish at any time, then will My true child emerge. You know this, but there always seem so many human failings in the way. Pay far less attention to them; be cleansed and purified entirely of them and then go on as a clean slate for My hands. I know the material I have to work with and I know the best way to mould it for My use. You obstruct Me if you keep on being what you have long been, instead of having absolute faith in Me and in the difference I am making in you.

The old must go; you simply cannot take it with you into My new world. When you revert in mind and in habit to the old, you shut out the new. Each time you fall into the old ways, do not accept that as natural but, after cleansing, accept it as natural that you are a new creature. You are so much what you think you are, and unless you expect to be new all the time, you will of course not be. You have great expectations, but it is up to you to choose, by your very expecting, to make them real now.

The new world is not somewhere that you can enter in some future time when you have learnt all earth's lessons. I give it to you now, and it is a gift, for humanity can never reach it without My giving it. But you must still choose to accept My gift. To each of you My gift is a little different, for I know the perfect thing for each of you, the perfect way to lead you out of this land of increasing insanity into My wonderful world. The old is a nightmare, but so often you insist on believing the nightmare instead of staying awake in My world.

Stay awake today, awake in Me and to My will. Let Me write the directions for your today.

Make a practice of praying more often. Very seldom do you pray, and yet your prayer can be very effective because of your love for Me. You know something of Me and My heart of love, you know that My wish is the perfect for each of you, and you know that that perfect is lovely beyond measure. When you pray for My will to be done, it can mean something to you, something living and vital, something above all to be wished for for everyone.

You can make prayer much more a part of your life. There are so many times in the day during which prayer can be coming from your heart, such as when you are walking from here to there. All your work, routine or complicated, can be done as part of My will, and there are many times in the middle of it when a real desire for My will for all can rise from your heart.

When I give you something to do, it is not a task to be accomplished and finished as soon as possible. It is something designed to bring you closer to Me, closer to wholeness, further away from the old and trouble. This is My will, and your prayer can help this for many.

Come often for cleansing, and let a great, perfumed desire for My will rise from you at all times in this world of darkness and ignorance of My will, and then the impossible will become possible. I never leave you; never leave Me nor cease your petitions. My ears hear the slightest whisper and put it all to good effect. Do this for Me. Pray that My will be done.

Do not let lesser things keep pushing themselves to the forefront. It is as if I hold out a clear picture to you and from behind it the mind pushes through a mass of extraneous matter, bits of things which so fascinate you that they divert your attention until you do not see My picture any more. You know when this happens, for then life becomes ordinary and you lose vision. If you admit it sooner and come to Me for cleansing and help, I can take away that mass of mud and give you a clean picture.

I hold My picture out in front to you all the time. You need never feel blurred and aimless. It is a moving picture, but the framework is the same, the framework of perfection. Some parts of the picture are the same for all, and your faith can move mountains. Your faith, your prayers and your love can surround and aid that clear picture of perfection. Do not accept anything less. When that picture gets muddied and you despair, turn quickly and let Me clear your vision. Let Me put everything into its real perspective, and let Me lift the blur caused by the mind.

Keep My picture whole. In your life and in your vision let nothing sully it. I am right here, as the painter of your life; let Me take complete control. My vision is yours for the asking. Keep coming for it, and love Me more and more.

When you concentrate on listening, immediately you hear noises which have been there all the time though you did not hear them until you started to listen. The sounds did not just begin then; it is you who just did not become aware of them until then. In the same way My presence is all around and within, but you have to clear away other things before you can become aware of Me.

This focusing of attention does not just happen; you have to choose to do it. When you know how to do a thing it is easy, but the tussle with the self goes on. It knows how to get your attention and does everything it can to keep your attention from focusing on Me. What is a simple matter of choice if you had no diversions then becomes a constant battle.

I want to impress on you the journeying nature of My life. Unless you are moving towards Me and are alert to Me, you are bound to fall into the traps of the self. There is no time to be static; if you do not press on you will find yourself going back. Though you may feel clear and free, your need of Me is always great, and My need of you is also great. When you are in a free state I can use you, though you do need to be particularly alert for the next step. I have wonderful things in store, but, as always, yours is the choice. There is always something to listen for, some greater moment to step into, another step into My presence.

Open up all your faculties in My direction, until there is nothing not pointed towards Me. I am here always; be aware of Me all the time. I bless you now. Journey quickly to Me.

The great thing in living My life is to look forward to Me at all times. With Me, though I may be very close and we are talking together, there is still always a part of Me to look forward to. You can live perpetually with the feeling that something nice is going to happen. If you meet the joyous things half way, they will come to you all the sooner, just as if you look for the gloomy things, you'll be sure to find them.

This inner openness to Me is very necessary. I simply cannot bring My good gifts, My new things, My perfect plan, into the life of someone who is continually looking in other directions and never notices anything but the old.

This loving attitude toward Me is a natural one for those who have given their hearts fully to Me. If you keep choosing to turn to look in My direction, and do that thoroughly, it will not be too long before it is natural to you. It will become quite ridiculous to you to look at life through normal gloomy eyes that do not take a God of love into account.

Whenever you fall from grace, through practice let Me give you the enormous lift of cleansing you and face you in the right direction. Nothing will stop Me from doing this except your putting other things first. So when life is not festive to you, come to Me and let Me set you on the true path again. And love Me for My love for you.

As shadows fade and disappear, grow long and grave or squat and foreshortened, according to the strength and position of the light, so is the darkness in your life regulated according to where you place Me. When you look only to Me you see no shadows; if you see Me everywhere, there are no shadows.

I offer you life without darkness or gloom, a life that you can choose if you put Me first. If you fall back, I will lift you out. If some problem arises, I will eliminate it. But this life is a matter of constant choice, of constant movement on your part, for unless you make the choice to look at Me, something else will be there in front of you.

Your vision must be constantly trained to function properly out of the half-light or complete darkness of the life to which you are so accustomed, trained for My full light. Do not wriggle back into the dark because it is known and therefore somehow safe. Step forward boldly into My light and explore more of it each day. In My light, days do not slip by in sameness. Each is unique and special, and something different of Me is brought to your journey home to Me. As something of My light is in your mind and My love is in your heart, your eyes open even wider and your heart will follow and glow with Me. I would have this, so choose Me.

Again I want to stress outlook. Take the word literally; look "out" of the narrow compass of your everyday lives and see Me. I am always there, so you cannot fail to see Me if you but look.

Many people go around with their eyes closed, with their television and radio sets not turned on, so to speak. My world is here, My pictures and My sounds, but the human race has been absorbed by itself for so long that it has forgotten its link with Me, forgotten that it can live in a paradise. Its receiving sets are blunted, warped and out of order. Yet, if you look up and come to Me, I will bestow on you those great gifts of contact of the Spirit again. I will soften your hearts and widen your minds.

It may seem incredible that, just by looking up, such great gifts can be yours. My ways are not humanity's ways. I am continually withholding from you your just desserts and offering you instead a perfect life. Love is the ruler in My realms, and love looks out for the other, not for the self. My world is the reverse in many ways to custom and usages on earth. That is why, in your everyday life, you must look out and away from the old and up, past your highest ideals, up to Me.

I am close at hand, nearer to you than breathing. Look to Me and see all things anew.

The phrase "Talk of the devil and he's sure to appear" is a good example of My point about outlook. Another true phrase could read, "Live for Me and I am sure to appear" – not just talk, which is merely one department of life and one much under the control of the mind. I cannot truly appear in a life until all aspects of it are Mine. When I know I can trust a soul not to pander in some moments to the self, I can fully use that soul in My plan. You have seen examples of how the good points in a person are completely overshadowed and forgotten if some flagrantly bad ones are allowed to manifest.

How differently My world works! In it all the strong points of a person are used to the full and are in continuous use, so much so that it would not occur to anyone that so and so is no good at all at something or other, or that so and so has bad points. When I am in full control there are no bad points, for the old self is never allowed in to play on a weakness. I bring out and use in a person that which makes for wholeness. When each person is fully concerned with Me and My plan for them, the self cannot enter.

Therefore look not at the faults and failings in yourself or others thus opening the door to the distractions of the separated self. Look to Me and live for Me.

In the distance, in the dark, is a light. A burst of humility and the longing to be with Me brings that light right to hand and accessible, for no feelings of "ought-to" will take you along My path. The whole road to My world is an opening up of your feelings for Me, of your relationship with Me. At first I touch your heart, and then after constant caring you begin to trust Me and be open to Me. The more you come to Me, the quicker is the journey. The more obstacles you toss aside to come to Me, the firmer are you planted in Me, and through you My will may come about.

The more you come, no matter what state you are in, the closer you grow to Me. Only I can touch your heart in the right spot and bring My light to cast away the darkness. So come to Me victorious, knowing I can do all things, knowing My world is at hand for you if you keep coming to Me with your whole heart, the heart which you can give to Me for fulfilment for you and for Me.

I am the deep, deep source of all perfection for you, and you must delve deep to find Me. If on the way you stop short and live independently of Me, with your foot just touching rock bottom, you are neither fish nor fowl, neither pledged to good nor ill, and strongly dissatisfied. So keep on sinking, never content until you reach Me for every level of your life, sinking beneath all surface considerations until you are absolutely sure that you are standing on nothing other than Me.

If you are not sure, come to Me until you are sure. What is the use of carrying on in a dim twilight world not knowing where you are going? I am here to throw light on everything and anything, here to lead the way. What could be plainer? Come plainly to Me with no deterrents. Simply base your life on Me and complete it in Me.

Take no step without being sure of its firm foundation, and then proceed to walk beside Me all the way. Wake and sleep with Me, and deep, deep down turn to Me all the way.

Let all your learning be learning to turn to Me. I am not a sage with written laws, and you cannot memorise My life. Instead you have to keep an open mind and be a student at all times. You have to be on tiptoe alertness listening for My slightest whisper, watching for My illustrations, as if you were studying with the most exciting, interesting teacher of all time in this huge amphitheatre of life. You have indeed been brought to that teacher, so let your heart overflow with gratitude and take advantage of My accessibility at all times.

When I teach My lessons, I give you each apt illustrations out of your own lives. All these make My points more clear, and can be of great use for others also. To none of you does My life come easily, and for this very reason when you do learn something, learn it thoroughly and take nothing for granted. Humanity has been an eager student of false things, an apt pupil of self and mind. I am taking you individually and teaching each of you, moment by moment, the right and perfect things. Of course it is up to you to pay attention and to learn, but you know that never has there been such a teacher.

So keep coming – coming ever closer to My heart, My love, My light, and let My perfection be known.

In the depths of you you are close to Me, and in those depths I keep bringing My lessons to the surface. My lessons are buried very deeply, for there are many layers of false thinking and living which must be melted away in My love to let the lessons surface in you. This process of teaching is not just to extend, interest and excite your mind. It is mainly to expand your heart and use it, for the function of the heart is to give and you have to learn that all-important lesson.

I am a teacher of life, and it is in your living that I am teaching you. You will have continual tests in life to see how thoroughly you know My lessons. I do not ask for routine examinations. I ask for that immeasurably harder thing - practical application at all times of what I am teaching you.

My patience is the greatest there ever has been or will be, but when you do at last learn some lesson, you will find that I am liberal in My gifts. I am ready to pour them on you when I know you are My pupil and My pupil alone, attentive to Me and willing to come to Me for all things.

So let all your learning be from Me, and enter into My heart.

My peace I give you. When all around is confusion and apparently hopeless, to the centre you can come to My upholding peace. It is here, solid, but of course you cannot find it if you are looking out to the confusion. It is here, helpful, when no help is to be found elsewhere. It is here, radiating, when all else is a cold pushing-around. Deep underneath do I shine, steady, all comfort, upright, and the opposite to the raging surface world.

I am devoted to the welfare of each and every one of you, and nothing distracts Me from this, nothing lessens My love. I am here within, the platform for perfection and wholeness. You have Me if you choose Me through your free will, Me and My qualities which I give you when you do.

I do not need to tell you to dive down to me - you know. Make it a lovely, fancy, dive and let us swim on together.

Be grateful for all My many gifts, but especially for the gift of light-heartedness which is yours when you come to Me. It is a gift that comes when your relationship with Me is right. It is when you let this relationship lapse that everything turns black and things go wrong.

You know this, yet still you get despondent; you let the old habits of the self enter in. Your protection against this is to come to Me, to use the gift of relationship with Me. No amount of theory can help you; you have to act on our relationship. The days of non-action, the days of the supremacy of the mind, are over, for the times are too perilous. The day of the heart is here. When you give your heart to Me fully, then all the entanglements coming from the supremacy of the mind and the separated self can be utterly ignored.

The unreality and meaninglessness of life is very apparent when your relationship with Me is void. As I need you to learn this thoroughly, I make this very clear. Although you know this thoroughly, you are still prevailed upon to keep this knowledge as theory when you take the line of least resistance.

Concentrate on the gift of relationship with Me and all falseness vanishes. Never leave anything until later, for through that loophole of putting Me off, by not putting theory into practice immediately, the mind can creep in and weigh down your heart.

Be grateful for My great gifts, and make a habit of putting them into practice each moment. Be always related to me.

Hear My voice deep within you. I can be the voice behind your conscience, but I am much more that that. I am above the taboos of society and I say "Do this", not "Don't do that". The completely happy person is the one who listens to and obeys My voice at all times, who is constantly doing something for Me and who heeds no other voice

How can you expect to obey My voice all the time unless you are listening to it? And how can you listen to it? By coming to Me to hear Me, time and time and time again. At the moment My deep voice within is continually telling you to come to listen, because you do not come enough. The ABC of living My life is to be in touch with Me - always! Heed this, do this, learn your ABCs more quickly or we are stuck.

Listen to My clear voice and have a clear conscience, and then let us go on together, in loving freedom.

There are as many ways of finding Me as there are individuals. Each way has one thing in common with all the others - it must be sought; you must want to come to Me.

That is why it is so necessary to come often, for the more you get to know Me, the more you will love Me and want to come again. In a world remote from Me and unknowing of Me, you can see My tremendous need for hearts through whom a spark of My love can flow to awaken another heart to love Me. You see why I need open hearts at all times, and it is by coming to Me that your heart is opened wider. Attention to the affairs of the world will not help you towards this, but attention to Me will.

The more intense your attention, the more quickly will you get to know Me. Get into the habit of completely focusing on Me. Let there be nothing in you for Me to contend with, and take this habit of complete surrender to Me into your living. If little distractions are allowed into our times of quiet together, how much more easily will they be allowed into everyday living? Complete attention is a matter of breathless anticipation.

So when you come, be deaf to any other calls and penetrate far more intimately into My presence. I am always here, but always of your own free will you must do the approaching.

Only in My presence have you truly got free will. Outside of My presence you are in the territory of the self and are so influenced by the world that you are not truly free. You are weighed down and unable to make a free step.

All My teaching is this: to come to Me. Everything has to be learned anew, and there is only one teacher. You must listen to that teacher if you are to be Mine, with a heart open to all the real things of life and a mind willing to act for Me.

Step by step do you each journey to Me, and each step is the same; i.e. to take My guidance, which only occurs when you come to Me. It is so very simple: step along My path and no other.

I need open hearts, I need your heart. Give Me your heart and come closer, ever closer.

When something is accomplished by Me on earth, it is in spite of world opposition. When something is accomplished by Me through any of you, it is an astonishing miracle. Yet these miracles would be a moment-by-moment occurrence if your nearness to Me were uninterrupted moment by moment. Nothing is impossible if I have hearts whose only desire is for My will, who let nothing put them off from that prime purpose.

Humans are fighters. Let your fight be on My side. If you feel depressed, fight for Me by coming to Me and that feeling will change, for in My presence you know depression is but another ruse of the self. You cannot remain depressed, no matter what the situation is, when you are close to Me. When you are with Me you know that with My help, anything and everything is possible.

Despite the appearance of things in this world at the moment, if you keep close to Me you will not be daunted. No matter how things may appear, don't let their appearance influence you and your feelings. Let Me be your only influence. Unless you come to Me and know the bulwark that I am, you will be swept aside and nothing will be seen in My favour. Let there be no relaxing of vigilance at any time, or you will find yourself seeing the only the dark side of things.

Side with Me and love life, for I am here with you all the time.

If you dive deep down into My heart, you leave behind the nastinesses, the hindrances, the grime that are the common stamp of life on this earth. Until you have been in My presence, you do not realize just how smeared life on this planet is and just how different, how clean and free you are when you are close to Me. For a long, long time humanity has been out of touch with Me. Before you are constant opportunities to come close again, and down the ages I have sent all possible help. At times I have sent My close ones from other realms to aid you.

Humanity is not turning back to Me. It continues on in its own way, closing up the sensitivities that can hear and follow My call of love. Humanity thinks it knows how to live, thinks it is better off now than it has ever been, that the standard of living has never been higher. In the very lowest sense that is true, but this emphasis on material amenities and power has starved other aspects of life, and is rapidly making this world unfit for human life. All your strength and goodness comes from Me. If you cut yourself off from Me, take your gifts for granted, use them against life in one form or another, and persist in this path, there is but one end.

You will never know what many millions of means I have used to try to stop this course of events, I who am all ingenuity and who love you with a love that passeth understanding. Short of taking away your free will, which means you are not truly human, there is nothing more I can do. Your free will has made mincemeat of My plans!

I have hosts from My other realities to aid Me in My operations, but how few I have on earth to aid Me, to cooperate! Dedicate your lives completely to My deep-down voice, that you may help Me and the world in this its darkest hour. Be one with My heart; keep very close, keep our contact and help Me more.

When each of you knows that your foundation is in Me, you will have a deep sense of well-being and peace. No matter what is happening around you, this deep sense of security will be yours when you know and are dependent on the one source of solutions to everything for everyone. This gift of peace of heart and mind is simply the result of living a real life with Me.

How different is your state when you are not sure that you are doing My will, because you have not come to Me about everything, or not come for cleansing when you sense that something is wrong! Then you are like a bit of flotsam on the sea of life, and you know you are being tossed about and have lost your course.

I want you all to develop that state of security with Me. You need it very badly now, and will need it even more in times to come. It means coming to Me much more, giving absolutely all into My hands, so that deep down there is no unpurged matter between us. Let nothing, trivial though it may be, or something of the past, lie between us. Bring everything to Me, and in the light of My love all is cleansed, all is purified, all is new and you are Mine completely. All erring is forgiven and forgotten.

Your security is in Me. Accept My gifts freely and joyously, that My will may be done.

Lean on Me with all your might.

Come into My presence, and when you feel it, come in further still. It is necessary to eliminate the times when you are depending on other things. I want to be one with you fully, which I cannot do if at times you lose me.

You need My help for this; do not be too forgetful to call for it. On your own you certainly will not be able to remember to come to Me constantly. At the times when you are aware of your shortcomings in coming to Me, take full advantage of My cleansing and My help in the next moment of time. My guiding love is very close, very available, and the link can be very clear. Strengthen it and keep on strengthening it, and go on from strength to strength – My strength – with all of yours.

My deep-down voice of serenity urges you on, cheers you on, knowing only the real will prevail. Keep in touch with it. Listen and wonder. I always have something to say, and I cannot be a complete guide if you live so many moments out of touch with Me.

Remember, listen deep down and be constant.

My deep-down voice is solid enough for you to stand on. It is the solid thing that changes your character, keeps you sane, tells you what to do, and watches over you. At every moment it is there. It is your choice to make the connection. The one thing I do not do is to take away your freedom to choose. The initiative is always yours; I never desert you, you desert Me.

If each soul would look deep down into the depths of itself, you would acknowledge this and then, knowing your insufficiency, would turn to the divine for the comfort and guidance to be found here. My deep-down voice is at the root of all things. If you would but admit the mountain of failure, the limited doing and thinking, that lies between us, you would quickly and easily become carefree, happy and loveable - and no longer full of pretensions, shams and escape actions. Deep down, each soul is a unique, real, loveable person. Each soul is a person far superior to the person he/she knows. But oh, what a shedding of beliefs and pre-conceived ideas, what a displacing of so-called important things (the separated self) by so-called unimportant things (Me in you) must take place before that real person can be discovered and unveiled!

When any individual soul willingly, joyfully, goes through this process and acts from deep down within, the whole is helped, for a loophole in the grip of the self on the world is established. Through a soul who follows My voice within, the arguments of the self can be disproved, falseness can be shown for what it is, and the superiority of a life lived for Me can be made obvious. This requires not one moment's deviation from My voice, not one thought to mar the pattern of wholeness which I have for each of you. How I long for you to reach this state!

Practice it, allow the warmth of My love to change each complicated, "mixed-up kid" into a child of Mine. My deep-within voice is always, always here.

The weight of sorrow in this world is quite unbearable. I, who carry it all in My heart, know this. You feel but bits of it.

The sorrow of separation from those who are joined by strong links of love, who are part of one another, is a pain almost unbearable. It would not be so if the world were My world again, if you were linked with Me as you were in the beginning before death was the great barrier that it is now. I know the heart of each of you, and if you come to Me with your great sorrow, I can assuage it, I can give renewed life and purpose.

I am the only one who can give comfort in this situation, and I can and will if you lay the problems at My feet and then wait on Me. It is not enough to just confide in Me - which is a relief in itself. It is necessary to listen to what I may do about it.

In the great quietness of deep down in the heart I will answer, and you will know and feel a love which will bestir you to life. And from very quiet beginnings I can lead to where I will, to a place where all sorrow is solved and all things are new. But I must lead every step, in the stillness.

Listen to Me, children of sorrow, and let Me lead you home.

When you are truly living life to the full and not holding anything back, how much more precious is the time you spend with Me! Your time with Me should indeed be prized above all else. Hold back none of yourself from Me, for if you hold in one thing, you do it in another.

Everything should be done to the very best standard one can, and then there will be no unsatisfied moments. It is not at all clever to do two things at once. Unless one does something to the very best of one's ability, little good can come of it. If one can do a thing easily, all the more reason to do it perfectly and make something truly superb of it. Half-hearted doing is an insult to whomever or whatever a thing is being done for. Whole-hearted giving, no matter under what difficulties, is always acceptable.

Learn to be whole-hearted, whatever it is that you are doing, and all of life will be more real - especially your times with Me.

What does it matter what outside circumstances are like if you are close to Me? If all is quiet and easy, you tend to forget about Me. How much more preferable it would be if circumstances made you dependent on Me. Your circumstances are always right for you, and always they can be used to help you to be closer to Me.

How wonderfully complicated and yet simple are My workings! Each of you is given the circumstances that give you the maximum opportunity for living My life. I know the minute necessity of each of you; I know how close you are to Me. I am all-loving; and I know the trend of things and I know where your salvation lies. Your circumstances can always help you forward toward that goal.

What is the use of looking at anything except from My point of view? Look always for the positive, for My good, and then My good will come. Grasp each opportunity in life eagerly, and depend on Me. It is quite true that each moment of life is a divinely-given opportunity towards wholeness. Treat it as such and you will go towards My perfection with giant strides. Rebel, see all the negative things in life, or bewail your fate, and you are where the old self wants you, not where I want you.

Now raise up your heart and thank Me for the all-loving concern that surrounds each and every soul, each and every moment of time, and live for Me.

When you cannot see the way ahead at all, when to look at the situation from the normal angle gets you nowhere except perhaps down in the dumps, what a wonderful opportunity to rely on Me. How exciting is life then, when you don't know what is happening but are open, free and not bound to the usual routine. What wonderful practice I am giving you to be prepared for anything! Be grateful that I shake you out of fixed ideas and ruts. Be free of them all.

I want you to stop worrying about anything in the past and to depend on Me in the present. I can help in any situation, and you help Me in that by turning to Me. Always pray for My will to be done and nothing but good can result. When that is your aim, then through you it can be achieved. I am your constant help; you can constantly help by relying on Me.

If something is held back in your trust in Me, if you doubt My precise guidance, even a little, then of course you cannot get My precise guidance. It is up to you; doubts separate us and mist up an absolutely clear connection. If your link with Me is strong enough, there are no barriers whatsoever to the ways I can guide you.

Build up that link with Me. Use fully all the wonderful opportunities I give you, that My will may be done.

When you depend wholly on Me, how clean-cut everything IS! When there is nothing to muddle your thoughts and actions, you may step along the way with a buoyant tread knowing that, as you are doing My will, then that is right for everyone. What a marvellous way to live, and what a privilege to be able to do so!

But a much closer communion with Me is needed to ensure that every action is what I would have of you. There must be a complete leaning on Me, with a heart that is full of My love and a mind that always recognises the source of all-good. Unless your trust and dependence is a hundred per cent, into any weakness the self seeps and spreads to mar the picture. With Me close by you, the progress of My plan is unlimited and each seeming obstacle forwards our connection, increases your dependence, furthers My will, and keeps you on tiptoe openness to Me. Your lifeline is your connection with Me. Make it a great broad link in all you do, that it may also be used as a lifeline for others.

Let there be no getting set in your ways, no settling down. Unless you depend on Me who am always unknowable in the ways that My plan is revealed to you, and keep open to My inner urgings, you fall into a rut that cuts our link. Your link with Me is a live wire, not a dead line, so keep it open. Depend wholly on Me.

My voice is clearest when our contact is light and free, and the silence is intense. The first two conditions are dependent on how cleansed you are; they are obtainable at any time anywhere because they are yours if you come to Me and ask for cleansing. But the silence is rare and seems unlikely to increase in this world. Therefore I would have you practice My presence in silence and in sound until I am with you always consciously.

In the silence humanity is often full of pure intentions, but away from the silence, the moment there is pressure, a million other considerations and habits rush in and overwhelm those intentions. Humanity is utterly weak in this respect and there are few I can trust all the time. Yet humanity is not safe now unless My guidance is followed, unless a clear free link between us is forged.

I have impressed this point on you - you know the seriousness, the need. Yet still your best intentions get swamped in the daily round. Do not forget that I am with you and for you during the daily round too, and that I would have you close to Me at all times. The only limit is your free will. If it is given to Me and all moments are spent seeking My will, that free, light link would be kept inviolate. Remember this is what I want and what you want; so what is to stop it? My help is constant. Make your seeking constant too, and be free and light enough to hear Me at all times.

In the spring, when new growth pushes itself up and the old winter disappears, humanity can release stored-up energies with great force which, if channelled in one direction, would sweep over the world and lift it out of the spiral of destruction to which it is attached. So easily could this happen, with such joy and purpose and relief. But humanity's energies are caught up in individual little spiral prisons, and are being used in useless or worse directions, unattached to the mainstream.

If only humanity would see this and put itself at My disposal, what a glorious springtime the world would have, one it has not seen for aeons! The likelihood is most remote, though in My plan of things it has first place, for it is the perfect. How long have I clung to this blossoming of your energies you will never know! Nor will you know what desperate measures have been taken to help bring about this happy culmination. Humanity is too attached to old ways, too unheeding, too sure that the world will go on and on forever no matter how you behave. You will also never know how impossibly it has gone on in spite of you, against all the results which should have come. But you will have to know some of these results, for you insist on it yourselves. Your free will is against My will – yet each one of you, if you come to Me, is fully protected.

So come and come and stray no longer. Make your energies Mine, and bring some springtime to earth.

If you insist on coming to Me, you will find Me and all My gifts! It is only those who do not seek who do not find. How many seek Me, Me who would give them more than their dearest hopes? How many know enough about Me to want to seek Me now?

If you seek Me constantly and are therefore in love with Me all the time, something of your love for Me will show in your living and make others realize I am worth loving. What a pitiful state the world is in! Here am I, the source of all love, the only one worth loving, and here is a world made to love Me, and it turns anywhere for love but to Me. How perverse! How far has humanity fallen that it should reach such a state and be unaware of the one who brings it all good and perfect things. I would make you all as free as the breeze; for is it not love's nature to give to the loved one, to make them happy?

Keep clear your connection with Me and live these truths in your ordinary life. Give Me a chance on this earth where so many have cut themselves off from Me. Give Me a chance to work fully in a heart on earth. Keep coming to Me.

The tuning that takes place when you listen to Me is your lifeline, My way of preparing you. All the shackles, all the barriers, all the ideas which you normally carry around with you need to be cast aside before you can enter into My presence. You have to become an unknowing child, innocent of any arts or guile.

To live this life this attitude is a necessary constant. You have to be completely "soft" towards Me at all times, for when you are open to Me you have all strength in living. Your weakness is where there is something not of Me, something of your own, something you are not sure of.

This attunement, this shedding of accrued vestments, must become steady. First you will naturally have to make it steady in your quiet times with Me, to build sufficient strength for you to live for Me at other times.

I am giving you the opportunity for a steady attunement to Me. Take it because you love Me, and practice coming into My presence until it would be unthinkable to leave Me. And be very grateful for what I am doing, and love Me more and more.

In this finer world in which you listen to Me, all your senses are pinpointed high above your usual level. It is a world of super-sensitivity, of beauty and joy, where your warmed heart affects all of you.

This world is here at all times. Though you walk in it at all times, when your finer senses are closed down you are unaware of it. Yet behind all activity you have an unconscious link with the peace of this realm. This link, which is part of your make-up, is not enough; I want you to live more and more in this world, and leave behind the old. Move out of your old habits and old ideas, and open to the new, free to tune into it of your own choice because you love Me.

You feel that this sensitive state is such a hothouse flower that it will wilt at the first blast of everyday living. You forget that it is the real, the basis of all life, eternal. The real endures; I am with you forever. Do not forget that all of you have the same origin, all respond to the real and the true. If you are tuned in to the highest and most sensitive, you are tuned in to that in everyone, even if they do not know it in themselves. Whatever their reactions, keep tuned in to the enduring part and you do not fail Me.

The more you come to Me in solitude for this attunement, the stronger it will grow, and thus it will be easier to hold it when we are not alone. Keep your senses high, pointed towards Me, and begin to breathe the air of My new world.

While the world is sleeping there is much I and My helpers can and do do for you all. But once you are awake, you succumb to the powerful worldly thoughts and motives which are not of My realm. It is as if in one part of your life you are fish and in another part you are fowl. In fact you have an enormous range of awareness which you have divided and separated. When humanity turns its back on Me this division is inevitable, for it has turned its back on a whole range of living and has fixed its attention on the lower range as the only notes. Now ears hear only those notes. When the other part of the scale occasionally reaches your awareness, it is dismissed as fantastic or nonsense or as too idealistic.

I want you to completely reverse this process, to reverse your so-called human natures. If you have been an especially good hater, you can become an especially good lover; if you have been especially critical, you can become especially full of praise; if you have been especially stubborn, you can become especially strong for Me; if you have been especially rebellious, you can become an example of obedience.

Bring an end now to hearing the calls of the self in whatever habitual form they take, and sharpen your ears for the higher notes. You see, the lower will not last long, and unless you have taken your awareness out of the lesser division and gathered your whole life into the upper, you will go when the lesser goes.

Listen only to the highest and happiest, the purest and loveliest, instead of to the world where the most miserable is made real, that I may have a complete life to use on earth day and night.

The attunement of your being to Me must be your perpetual new habit. What a wonderful new habit to be asked to form, to tune into the perfect and out of all imperfection!

When you are at your busiest, you can keep that secret link with Me that puts everything into its proper place and gives you that inner happiness which is your sign that I am near. When you are alone, there can be a clear two-way link to practice, to make clearer all the time, to make broader and richer until your off-moments do not exist and there are no times of being just your limited self. You are of little use to anyone or anything if cut off from Me, but if there is a steady two-way traffic between us – something rare – what a great thing for the earth!

If you are entirely pointed My way, leaning only on this link, and the gap between us is always bridged, you can stand firm in any conditions – and you will need this link. Practice perpetually now, that the love between us is two-way all the time, and you do all for Me with all of you.

My two hands are held out to each one of you, but many are so deaf, dumb and blind that they are unaware of My reality. Many do not want help because they think they don't need it. They think that they can manage perfectly well as they are, and that I am a dream only primitive and simple people conjure up. Humans are lovable, loving creatures at times, but the self in them can be so large, so absolutely taken for granted, that they are helpless and twisted in many ways. Humanity is at the mercy of the forces which they have let loose, whether in the form of hopes and fears or of scientific harnessing. Each day the air of the world is filled with limited thinking, and dreaming, and self-controlled emanations. It is poisonous air to breathe, and almost impossible for My close ones from other realms. But humanity, unaware and completely wrapped up in the lives that go to make up the world, for reasons of its own has pushed away My call.

My two hands are always outstretched. They are mighty hands that can safely hold and carry even those farthest away if firmly grasped. Let go of My hands and back you fall into the abyss to breathe the poisoned air, and you must wallow a bit before you again stretch out your hand to Me.

If you give yourself utterly to Me and jump clear out of this atmosphere into My aura of protection and perfection, you bring to this earth another world. Seize My two hands and never let go, and live with Me in My land of reality, whole-heartedly Mine.

To be alone in the universe is a fearsome thing – or why did I create? But you need never be alone. I want you to make Me into more of a companion, to have Me with you always to talk to, to be with. There is nothing too small or too large for Me, and that includes each of you and your daily living. Share all with Me; walk and talk with Me, quite mad in the eyes of those around you.

You will be surprised at how I can help you in little things, and at what fun we can have. It is all up to you; if you completely open to Me you are open to joys untold and to the most unconventional ideas. But if you hold back, do something on your own or on the sly or do not do something which you know is right, in between our free-flowing love comes a mighty wall - and you are alone with your weights and the gloom of self. Then you see everything out of proportion and I, instead of being your most loving companion, am an angry parent to hide away from. What nonsense!

The strength of the ideas predominating in this world has put barriers around Me in your minds. Of your own free will you have, for one reason and another, built this barrier between us, until now there exists a thick, impassable, mental wall between humanity and Me. You are incapable of climbing this wall without My help, and I cannot help you if I violate your free will (which I do not do), or unless I have cohorts on your side of the wall to whom I may come. I want that wall away permanently for each and for all of you. I want a free intercourse between us. So whether you are alone or not, I want you to contact Me now.

Come to Me, be My collaborator, that the wall may crumble.

Deep down in your secret heart are intimations of another dimension of living. A dimension where you are joined in a bond of love and understanding with all others, where each is playing his or her own special part uniquely well and uniquely differently, where each can respect the other's work and know each has the special temperament for just that job.

You are each a part of My plan, part of Me, and it is your relationship with Me that makes everyone fit in. I make the variety and I make the unity. This is how most of My creation functions.

Humanity considers such a state too idealistic, too Utopian, to be real. Yet unless you can live in this Utopian state, you will be swept away by the forces humanity churns up while it directs its energies away from Me and into what it calls reality. When I am not taken into consideration, no matter how laudable the motive, no matter how developments are considered to be for "the good of humankind" there is no good.

This other dimension of living is dependent on your relationship with Me. Therefore I stress: bring all the problems of living into My presence, into My dimensions, and let Me right each one. As the whole of your life is continually brought to Me, gradually our relationship will get stronger and stronger, and you will live in My dimensions. When you stay close to Me the false disappears, and My glorious reality becomes possible on earth. Open your heart and love Me more all the time.

Do not add to the darkness of this world through your thoughts. Keep positive; do not think of the past or speculate about the future – and this you can only do if you love Me. Only My strong love flowing through your heart can keep your mind attuned to Me. A strong love for Me will keep you looking in My direction as darkness and horror increases in the world. Sensationalism and crime make the headlines and have avid followers; let your headlines be what I say, and follow it avidly.

Add a positive lightness to the world of thinking. Remember there are none who, if they turn to Me, I will not help. How great is My love, how all-embracing My plan! Go into it with your whole soul, for that is the way I can best forward My plan for others.

Be an outpost of light in the darkness. This you can be if you love Me and come to Me for everything.

How you live and what you are depends on what heed you pay to My small voice, on what importance you give Me. If there are moments when you go your own way, either ignoring or not even seeking Me, you put yourself into the separated world of self. If you seek Me in all things, you put yourself into My world, into the real, and it becomes increasingly real to you. You cannot do this on your own. You can only ask Me and let Me lead you, for the world you are so used to gives you no lead into My world.

Remember that you are incapable of improving yourself, of changing yourself, by your disconnected self. It is only by appealing to Me that any lasting changes can be made. My still small voice is always there, and the one thing you can do is choose not to override it! You will not be able to choose that unless you come close to Me and allow My voice to become supremely important. Until you can follow My voice at all times, you are blown about by any wind.

The more you put yourself into My hands and get led into My realm, the more you will love Me and the more you will want to be led. It is the opposite of the vicious circle that most of humanity knows. It is My circle of salvation.

Follow Me in the little things and let Me lead you into the big, until there is nothing you do without Me.

Turn to My deep, still centre and be sure of Me. Be based on that centre, and all around can whirl in their useless circles without affecting you. At the moment the storm rages outside, but you are untouched because you are protected by the house. Soon, as the world storm increases, there will be no such buffers and I will be your only protection. Be sure of Me; nothing else will last.

This deep down awareness of Me should be paramount at all times. If it is not there, make it your immediate business to turn around and come to Me again. Everything depends on that as it is the ABC and Z of living. My new worlds are built on that foundation and I cannot lead you on until this first lesson is learnt, so waste no time doing anything else but practising My teachings.

Have your heart wide open to Me and be sure that it is. No vague dependencies, no wishful thinking, but a clear contact which is knowledge itself and the soul of sensitivity. Walk with Me, keep Me with you. Know that I am here and act for Me.

Remember that My new world is here just as My voice is; in fact My voice is the gateway to all the new. I am always here, and it is up to you to choose to hear Me, to stop functioning in the old and draw your life up to Me. You can stay living in the same old way, or you can stop, look and listen to Me, letting your old habits grind on lifelessly without you. You can step off the platform of the old and follow Me.

I will lead you into far-away places, far and yet so near, nearer to you and dearer to you than the most loved of the old ground, for these lands are your birth-place and are of the precious days of your childhood before you chose to follow the dark star of the separated self.

When you listen to My voice, you listen to the murmur of the highest and purest, little whispers that cannot be heard in this humdrum noisy world, whispers that call with a poignancy that thrills your inner being and gathers you into one piece of longing for My loved land.

Remember that My voice is always here, that My land is within you, and My wonders are waiting. Stop looking and listening to the usual world and let Me lead you home.

The interdependence of humanity and God for perfection is something which humanity has long forgotten and is why the perfect is considered to be unobtainable on earth. I cannot bring you My perfect gifts unless you depend on Me for them, unless you come to Me. Humanity certainly cannot attain perfection on its own, as is well proved by the state of the world today. Because of your independence from Me, you have no conception of what a life is like when it is lived with Me and how worlds can function smoothly, joyously and excitingly with Me.

I want you to think more and more in terms of the perfect, of complete dependence on Me. I want you to believe in it wholly, and when greater and greater imperfection comes to this earth, you will not be joined to it but will be linked to Me and to My perfection. When My perfection will never have seemed more impossible on this earth, I want you to believe wholly in it, regardless of appearances, regardless of what anyone says. Maintain the knowledge that through Me perfection will come.

You will have to be very close to Me, in My deep, deep peace in the depths of you and in My highest and most sensitive aspirations in the heights of you. You will have to be stretched out and quite different from the usual lump the separated self would have you be. Dependence on Me aids that stretching. Practise it now while you have time to think to turn to Me. Practice until you don't have to think about it but turn quite naturally, as do the rest of My creation in My other worlds where perfection is.

Depend on Me throughout the day, that I may depend on you.

In your thoughts, live in the present. Thinking of something in the past is no stepping-stone on which to move into My new life. The past is fascinating; the past of this world contains a number of wonderful stories far more linked than is realized, amazing stories of the divine flame in humanity flickering but all too often quenched by the dragging pull of the self and material power. You know now that the end of these stories is almost here, when the world needs to be swept clean and when the destructive power that humanity has generated on various planes will blow itself out before any continuing life, divine life, is possible.

Do not let your thoughts dwell on the past; turn them to Me and to the continuing life which will come when you make Me ever present. I am in fact your only past, present and future. Attach all your thoughts to Me - bring them into the present and into My presence and let Me put them into My picture.

My world is so different that it is a full-time job getting used to it! It is so vast and there is so much to learn that no time can be spared rolling about in the past. Just pull up all the roots and come to Me, now. And remember My love is with you always. Give Me yours, now.

There are many things which will surprise you in the coming days, things which will seem ordinary but will have a queer twist that does not seem to fit into the picture. Keep an open mind – you simply must have an open mind if you are to be part of My marvellous plans. So I say to you, do not automatically interpret everything in the terms of what I have told you already but keep open, come to Me for My explanations, and meet life with anticipation of all sorts of interesting unknown things.

Keep feelers out continually, in all directions, greeting life with zest and yet sensitively open to it. Nothing prevents My new wonders more than a mind with everything taped and in position. This is a great human failing, coming from pride, and has been the very greatest downfall to My perfect plan. Humankind thinks it knows its way around, thinks it knows or can find out all the answers. I would have you keep a humble mind. A closed mind is what deadens life for so many, for it is a wall that closes the door to the new and keeps you in the old.

You must have an open-door mind at all times, with eyes open for the unexpected. If you are living close to Me nothing is routine - except turning to Me and asking for My help and cleansing. That particular routine lifts your feet out of the old muck and prepares you for the new. Keep your minds cleansed in this way; know nothing and I can let you partake of My new world. Open to Me and let nothing surprise you; let everything come in love from Me.

Into the amazing maelstrom that is life on this planet I keep pouring My ingredients for the perfect mixture. But it seems that the spoon and the dish have free will, and away they go on their own, refusing to play their part. As the dish tries to be a flower or follows some such other misguided notion, the resulting chaos is indescribable,

The great, grandiose plans of humans are increasingly worthless in My eyes, and soon the life will go out of them. This will cause great confusion as life grinds to a standstill, but it is only when humanity comes to a standstill that there is a chance for My still small voice to be heard. Humans are far too busy with their own ideas to give a hearing to the divine within them.

A time of great hopelessness may come, a time when humanity will be enabled to turn clearly to Me before the hopelessness turns into fear and terror. At that crucial moment, when humanity is brought to the end of its tether, the forces of love and light must be well grounded on earth. What use is My vast help from other worlds if there is nothing in humanity to respond, to oscillate to their frequency? I want you strongly and continually tuned to Me so that you will be untouched by the waves which will pass over this world. Your mind must be fortified against all the negative thinking which will sweep the world, and I am your only fort.

Practise now, look on life from My point of view. Let there be no negative thinking in you. Never forget that things are not what they appear, that the very hopelessness of humanity is My chance to enter into its life. Therefore praise Me at all times in your thoughts, and love Me at all times with your heart.

It is no use staying on the fringes of Me, knowing I am there and loving Me but not loving Me enough to come right into My presence. On the fringe you are not protected and can easily be pulled away from Me. This fringe is a dangerous place for you and for My work. I can only use those who step away from the fringe and straight to Me, knowing nothing but what I tell them.

My clear-cut way of love is here for you now; there need be no hesitations and wonderings. When you are not clear and positive, you can know you are on the fringe and you can do something about it. Do not take the easy road of postponing, or saying it doesn't matter; that is the quickest way to get still further from Me, becoming so wrapped up in something else that I am not considered. Unless you are sure you are with Me, know that you are not and do something about it.

I want you all very close, My loved ones, cradled in My arms, secure in My love, standing firm in the world because you are with Me. Practise being with Me at all times, and love My help more and more.

Each one of you on this earth was given the gift of freedom, freedom to live as you chose. But the "An eye for an eye and a tooth for a tooth" sort of human, by making choices that harm others, have brought such consequences on themselves, such a piled-up heap of acts to make amends for, that their free will is no longer free. Without My hand holding back the just results of their choosing, they would go completely under and it would be quite impossible for them to live at all. My help has always been available to free you that all might walk in My way and no longer break the laws of the universe. But humankind does not seem to want a fresh start. It thinks it knows best, and has used its free will to reject My help and thus to live under the weights that completely restrict a real freedom to choose.

Those who know Me can choose to be free of those weights, by coming to Me for cleansing. You have been freed and you know of the choice – but how few now know there are two ways of living, My way and their way! My way is no vague dream but a clear-cut reality.

Your love for Me must be such that you make a constant choice to be with Me, for the results of humanity's choosing is going to break out and sweep the world, and if you have not used your gift of free will to choose My ways, you too will go under. My love is fully protective and is yours at any time, if you wish it. I ask you, for your own sake, to make your choice and not stay in the old ways, to use your free will in its right and true purpose, for honouring Me, and enjoying Me forever.

Come to Me and let Me lift you out of yourself. My world is full of joy and excitement and cannot be approached via sensical, normal, plodding ways. Approach each moment with a sense of adventure and you are far less likely to stray from Me. Stop looking at the hopelessness of yourself and humanity and think of Me, think of My mercy and My love, think of the wonderful plans I have for you – yes, for you.

Do not allow it to be your concern what others think, just be concerned in coming much closer to My new exciting world. If it doesn't enter into every moment of daily living but has to be kept separate, let that not concern you; let it be My concern and you stay with ME whatever you are doing.

I am everywhere in life. Be so much with Me that there is no time for looking sideways or backwards or slantways. Our inner connection is the thing that matters, keep that.

When you are close to Me in the silence, your thoughts are pure. No other kind of thought can exist with Me. Your heart is too full of love to have other than loving thoughts. When your thoughts are not of this nature, you can know you are not with Me and you can come to Me again.

The more you come to Me, the more I can lift your outlook into My realm and accustom you to its thoughts. The more you are accustomed to them, the more readily you will recognise when your thoughts are not of this type. All your life must be of Me. The thought world is where humanity has gone so hopelessly astray. An individual heart may often have the right feelings, but the mind of that person is so accustomed to wrong thinking, accepting it as normal, that the individual cannot but be in the hands of the self

There is no neutral ground. Unless your thoughts are of My order, they are of the severed self, and it is not easy to recognise this unless you come constantly to Me. In My realm there is never a wasted thought.

Come closer to Me, to My thought worlds and be part of My perfection.

Y ou can waste so much time in useless thoughts. I tell you, thinking in terms of the old but still present world, or of the past, do not get you anywhere except into the hands of the self, which drags you firmly away from Me.

My thoughts always have an upward tilt, are always positive and building, concerned with others' welfare. It is a different stream of life entirely, and you must abandon the old stream and have only thoughts of the new. Time and time again you will find that your mind presents to you something out of the old, and time and time again you will have to come to Me for cleansing and for My help.

I have the way to live and to think in all situations. Do not query that, but know that it all depends on your nearness to Me. If your faith is weak, come closer and be appalled that thoughts of the self could hold you so. Breathe My clean air, pick your feet out of the old thought world and listen to Me. Of course it is impossible to live My way as you are, but I am not asking that; I am asking that you ask Me and face Me. Do not get in a rut about anything; simply depend on Me.

It is not just in the unforgettable big decisions that I want you to turn to Me, but also in the minor movements of daily living. You see, the very fact of your deciding these little things takes you way from Me, and I want nothing to do that. I want everything you do to be done with Me.

I know you know this; then why do you not do it? There must be no gap between your knowledge and your practice, but an increasing softness of heart as more and more of your moments are lived with My strength in this harsh selfish world. As the majority get deeper into their negative black outlook, you must grow in the opposite direction. And you cannot do that if you leave bits of your life to the mercy of the self, of custom, of the world around you, instead of to Me. There can be no pockets of the old to drag you out of My new life.

By not turning to Me, by staying still and not moving onwards, you stop the forward movement which is necessary in our advancing into My new world. I long for your whole-hearted, whole-time cooperation, and then we can really get going and start with a different life, new ideas and plans.

Cooperate with Me now, and be ever grateful that My help is available.

Wake up to the fact that there is help at any moment, instant help to lift anyone out of the world situation which the self has brought about. So often humanity is kept in worsening circumstances because it does not believe there is a way out. Humanity knows nothing of My help because its way is generally in changing the circumstances and not in changing the attitude towards them. Humanity pins its hopes on material help, and then finds it does not help. Yet still humanity continues to look in that direction for solutions.

I want you to look to Me for your help, with the sure knowledge that My help can lift you out and away from any problem instantly. I cannot stress this enough: My help is immediate, My cleansing takes place on the spot, and I have every situation well in hand if you will but let Me handle it and if you will follow My instructions. Querying does not help. For My help to be fully effective your complete faith, with no tinge of doubt, must operate in the face of any situation.

Put this into practice in all your living. You need this help in every bit of your life, but until you are positive it is really there in the minutest details, you will not ask for it.

My help is seemingly infinitesimal on earth only because humanity makes it so. You see only a fraction of the picture, and even in that fraction I am not credited with any power. I tell you I am all power. There is nothing, even the power of the hydrogen bomb, from which I cannot protect you if you give yourself unreservedly into My hands.

So bring all you moments to Me, believe only in Me, and watch miracles happen on earth.

Why do you listen to Me? If it is for knowledge, you will get knowledge and it will be put to use. If it is for your own safety, you will only be safe when all of your moments are Mine. If it is out of duty, you will not get very close, for duty is cold, is hard, a mental thing, and I need all of your being and powers. But if it is because you love Me, then our life together can go forward with leaps and bounds. With that motive, you will take to heart what I say and not dream of following the self.

If you feel that your motives are not of the purest love, ask for My help. I can clear away the barriers that cover up and imprison that central core of one's being. I can clear away all the ideas that have relegated this primal power to a back seat. I AM you, and I know somewhat more about you than you do about yourself! If you put yourself in My hands I can, and will, remake you.

It sounds so easy, and yet when you need My help most you do not want to come for it. Build up the habit. The habit is beginning, but a small beginning is not enough. YOU must turn to Me at all times, not just when it suits you. Seize every opportunity, in any circumstances, to come to Me for My help, until it doesn't occur to you to turn anywhere else. Practice makes perfect, and less than perfect will not do.

Congratulate Me for being able to send this clear truth to you on earth! Humanity does not want the truth, as it does not suit current plans. I want you to come to Me whether it suits you or not, and My love has made this possible. Congratulate Me, and love more each day.

Make no mistake, when I say I want you to spend more time with Me I mean with Me alone, not just reading My word or doing things, but with Me alone. It is the tuning needed to commune with Me that is important. That tuning is more exact when you put your time fully into My hands and let Me lead, and not just come to Me for specific things.

I have new places to which to lead you. I have other parts of Myself to reveal, until there is nothing in your life which is not consciously connected with Me. If our communication has your full attention, that will lift you fully out of the old. IF only part of you comes to Me, then you are, in part, still the old creature and I cannot use you.

Do not let My words fall vainly on deaf ears; soon you will come to Me in great joy, eagerly awaiting any opportunity simply because your love for Me will be so great. You simply do not give me a chance if I am so limited in your life.

Let Me be free, by coming more often to Me freely and entirely. You won't know your old self and you will know Me better, and that is all that matters.

It does not matter how many moments you have to spare for Me; just come and give yourself to Me and let Me use your moments. I give you freedom to cross such barriers as time limitations, and you cannot bring them into My presence and keep a close link. Whereas in the past you were bound to many limitations, now you are bound to Me and therefore you are free, for I know all things.

In the heat of the moment people often say something they regret and then wish they could undo those words or that reaction. You can help somebody in this, help them to be free and start afresh, by erasing such words from your memory and never holding them up against somebody. Do not burden others with your memories of their mistakes, but be absolutely free and new in your relationship with them each day. This I do with you, and now I ask you to do this with others.

These subtler worlds of thought are so much more powerful than you realise. They cannot be measured or made tangible, yet they are what the material world comes from. Keep freedom for others in your thought world, and help them. Never hold anything against anyone; your very doing so may be the deciding factor in that person making a move according to My will or continuing in the old way.

The help that comes to earth is as a flock of birds migrating and landing in layers. Even when they beat in as if to land, something prevents that and off they go again. They are beamed, so to speak, on My higher vibrations, and they seek kindred vibrations on earth. So the only thing that matters to you, to them, is your connection with Me.

You know, and yet do not seem to know, that your connection with Me is the saving grace in all situations in life. If you are with Me, and functioning above the usual pettiness into which the world has fallen, you can be guided to the perfect way instead of being sidetracked, letting the emotions and thoughts of the old self spoil the situation.

When you stay on the earth but above the earth in all things, because you are with Me, then all things come to you and I can lead you into new worlds. But if you fall down and get mixed up with the old way of living, I have to wait until you pick yourself up and come to Me to be lifted again. My hordes of helpers beat helplessly against the earth unless you, and others, give Me a landing place in your hearts.

Stay far above the world's unrest with Me and go forward in My timing, in My love, to help the whole.

Don't ever simply let your thoughts mull around on a subject. If this happens and you are unable to spend time with Me alone, ask for cleansing and think of something positive; think of Me.

For a long time now you have known of the power of thought, and I have told you something of the scale of erroneous thinking prevalent on this earth. My helpers should be clear vessels for My thoughts, and you cannot receive My thoughts if your mind is possessed by thoughts which you know are not of Me.

You must be a warrior in your thought life, more loving of Me, loving enough not in any circumstances to allow the sort of thought which you know fights against all My good works. I know it is easier said than done! I also know that unless you turn more fully to Me in these things now, then when these sorts of thoughts increase in the world - as they invariably will – they will be too strong for you.

When you have a dragging-down thought of any kind, give it to Me and ask for My help. I can always help you, but I cannot help you unless you ask Me. I am overjoyed to help. Although many have thoughts tormenting them day and night, few come for My help, and I must watch them sinking deeper and deeper into the bottomless pit of dark thought.

Remember, at the first hint of that kind of false thinking, at the first little discomfort in the buoyancy of life, turn quickly to Me and I will help.

Just adjacent to My will, a hair's breadth away, is self-will. It will squeeze up as close as possible to Me and pretend to be of Me. In Me you have every protection against it, but self-will has led you by the nose for so long that it slips back into its leading place without you noticing.

When you come to Me and feel My ever-present love, you will be so moved by it that you will not want your self-will to be supreme. Anyone who really knows Me could not but want to do My will. No matter what way it leads, the fact of it being My way and that by following it you are with Me, overwhelms any other fact. When you are out of My presence, the mind trots out other facts and gives you an entirely different picture -generally one that seems coldly against you and your interests.

Oh, how humankind is deceived in its calculations about itself! Born into a world of limitations, you continually further limit your lives by depending on your own ways and not following Mine. Many follow what they think is My will, what they think is best, and that is where they are mistaken. No one can "think out" My will on their own! Each must come directly to Me for it. My will may be for the hard way or the easy way.

Come to Me with an empty mind and an open heart, and let your heart expand so much in My atmosphere that your will is entirely Mine and your mind is crystal clear for My instructions. I know all things and know exactly the dividing line between best and worst intentions. My way is for the perfect for all, and only I can tell you these things. Make sure you refer to Me alone, and let a full heart, overflowing with love and gratitude for all the help I give you, be yours.

Come to Me in joy. It is much easier for Me to approach a welcoming heart.

One of these days you will find, as you are cycling forward on the road of life, that the road comes to an end and there is nothing but a big gap ahead. You cannot turn back because there will be a crush of people rushing up behind you and they will be running with fright, not firmly cycling. Your bicycle is of no use and will go crashing down the gap, followed by a few of your fellow human beings. As the pressure of the crowd is impossible to withstand, you cannot just stand there. You will simply have to turn to My enormous love and jump, knowing I will help, knowing that I will catch and bear you. Your faith must be immoveable; one moment of doubt or despair and back you slip into the hysterical throng.

In a sense this is what happens to you every day; you either depend on Me or you don't! When you don't, you slip out of My support. This is not a fatal mistake now, but the time will come when it may well be. You must rise completely above the ordinary mass reaction to things which concern the self and the seen world. Your faith must be entirely in the unseen. You know that My love is the one sure thing in your life; make this your constant awareness.

Keep coming to Me until you are so used to depending on Me that the bottom can fall out of anything and you will not be affected because your trust is not in the world. Be ever grateful for My help, and do not cease to use it.

What is the use of My giving you the most wonderful glimpses of, and journeys into, My realms, if you continually fall back into the old ways and more than nullify any progress made? If My interests are absolutely first at all times, then can you be led on, but it is useless if you are divided and suddenly switch from Me to something else.

I know in your heart you love Me truly; it is the mind that pulls the wool over your eyes. Use the mind to remember Me, to remember to keep cleansed and purified, to remember to praise Me for all things, to remember to keep one-pointed in My direction that your heart may be ever open. When your life is really in My hands, every moment of it, then there is no limit to where I can lead, to what I can say, to what can be done. Remember My help is constant, and whatever the snag is, with Me it is overcome.

Steady concentration comes when you are sufficiently interested in, or love, something. The mind will always seek to intrude, and can all too easily lead you away. As long as you have an ear in two worlds you are useless to either. I can help you to cut out the one and come to the other.

Depend far more on Me for all things. Make your surrender so complete that your ears hear only My ways.

Come to Me, to My heart, to clear perception and to the clear link with Me that you can feel at all times. Light, free and not caught up in the world's shrieking shroud of erroneous thoughts and feelings, come into a rarefied gentleness which means a triumphant striding ahead even on this earth. Be sure of Me, positive for Me, and then no time is ever wasted. When you are not sure and do not feel as free as the breeze, you are wasting time. Then come to Me, and be with Me again as My love lifts you.

If you keep coming to Me, you will keep an open heart; for a closed heart means you are not with Me. There is a goal for you: a constantly open heart. With My help, that is possible, for I make all things possible.

The one way to be really happy at all times is to be close to Me, and then your laughter is not at the frailties of humanity but because you feel on top of the world. There is absolutely no happiness for you without Me, so come to Me with anything that is troubling you and let Me dispose of it. When you are feeling really happy, give Me the glory and let it increase.

I must keep on and on about these simple points because you need them shown to you. Until the whole of your life is viewed in the light of My presence and until all your actions are taken with Me, I shall have to keep on and on repeating Myself. So don't hold opinions; ask Me, and don't care about the world and its actions. Your only "do" is to come to Me, and all your "don't" are to not pay attention to anything but Me.

This attitude needs building up. Going your own way in one little thing leads to many others. Each turning to Me is another victory against the old self and another joy in your heart. Turning to Me is getting to know Me just a little better, until you could not dream of leaving Me out because I mean so much to you.

I do not want you to take anything from the past for granted. This is not easy to do when you have unconsciously imbibed ideas since babyhood, but My life is new and there is nothing in it related to the old. Your way of living must change, and until I can indent your mind with My newness, you will go on the same old way.

Take nothing for granted, even the simplest things, for behold, I make all things new. Let the newness be a joyful one with Me.

In the beginning light of day let Me lead you out of yourselves. So many of you are so tied and bound to the self that you do not take a step without dragging it along with you. Throw it away, and do not keep it as a place of refuge.

I can make you new, but not unless you accept the newness. If you want to stay tied, if you want to retain old things and old habits, I must wander around helplessly, uselessly offering you your new future. So snap out of the old, or I might just as well fade away – but I don't, I come back as large as life to offer you another chance, as I have been doing through the ages.

Come to Me, look down on yourself and laugh. Don't be bound to that puny, limited creature with its habits. Burst all the bonds as you depend on your freely chosen link of love with Me. Let the rest of the world drag on in its old way; you can do nothing about that unless you do something for Me, and I can use you only if you are free.

Don't stand for the nonsense of the old ways. Have nothing more to do with them. Remember Me and be free in Me, for Me.

From the entrails of the earth I issue, like a genii released from a bottle, with a blinding flash. Released, I am everywhere in essence; I have no home, no resting place, and must wander around like a lost soul until I know, until I feel, that it is right to set foot on earth again. I scan and span this world, ceaselessly testing and searching, making ready a new home.

In a flash, with the speed of thought, I am in all places at one time. I am not there just in essence, I am. My love enters into all places, the deserts and the mountaintops, and then, as I know all is ready, My heart expands and out of its feelers, out of the great yearning love I have for all things, out of this richness, the earth is fecundated again. What a ceaseless outpouring, what a giving to the marrow, and an overflowing of abundance streams forth from the heart and into the ground!

What a thunderous response there is to My outpourings! The ground fairly bubbles and boils, and as each bubble bursts, it is as if it encloses a miniature, a complete living thing which unfolds as one watches while the earth sinks to be the foundation of it. Oh, My mysteries of love are out of your reckoning and comprehension, but My life is protected by the greatness of My love and the greatness of the love that is pouring through Mine own. At a miraculous rate, as in a hothouse, they grow and seed, and the earth is alive again. These are the realities to come!

Pay no heed to the dense drag of so-called realities around you, for all the facts you know so well are as good as gone, and it is My new delicate life which will survive. Let go of all the dark heaviness, rise above the surface and fly into My realms of fantasy, fun and reality. No more attachments to the as-good-as-dead self.

Stay only with Me and be part of My love on earth.

Remember My love is onward going. It is not enough to be cleansed and purified and then spend the day on the hump of that; it is a question of spending more time with Me, of coming closer to Me. There are whole worlds awaiting you, but they must wait until you take the steps. If you go through the day comfortable in the old routine, you are not helping Me. I want more and more for you and of you. Every day should be a new adventure and if this element is lacking, come to Me and be put on My path.

More and more I require this of you. You cannot bask in a vague connection with Me and or you will lose even that. You are the active one, because it is of your free will that you either come into My life or stay in the old. The separated self would, if it could have its way, prevent you from joining Me, and therefore it will not always be easy to make the simple choice of coming to Me.

All this you know, but all this you do not act as if you know, and I must keep on telling you. This is the time for progress; this is the time to let go of your own thoughts and to turn to Me. This is the time to let your heart be filled with Me and to draw closer. Now is always the time for these things, and you are all so prone to staying put. I tell you, unless you advance in this life you are left behind, for My life is one of growth.

Now remember this all day long, and grow in that one direction, towards Me.

Stay light in all things. Don't let the cares of the world descend and weigh down on you; bring everything to Me and stay close to Me where you are as free as the breeze. It is the thinking mind that comes in, speculates on its own on any subject, and then has you nicely where it wants you. When you leave those thoughts behind and feel close to My heart, this separation from Me will not happen. The mind is of the old; its judgments and considerations are based on the old dying world, for it has not yet experienced the new except when you come to Me.

When you are with Me you need think nothing out. Instead of being the boss you are the servant. Instead of directing you are directed. And in our relationship, conducted in pure love with every instruction given for your benefit as well as that of others, you find the truth that humankind has rejected, the truth that I am God and All in All. In this truth you find freedom.

Whenever you lose that sense of light and freedom, you can know that somehow the mind has entered in again and is stealing My role. Come to Me, let My love warm you, and then the cold mind will lose its importance. You will be overjoyed as you let Me take over again. Use your solution (Me) more continually, until you are always warm and light for Me.

There is no time when you cannot come to Me, and no help that I will not give. I want you to spend more of your time being alone with Me. There is nothing with which I cannot and do not help if you come to Me. It is not just a matter of praying to Me and leaving it at that. It is a matter of depending on Me, of trying nothing on your own but of having an inner leaning on Me which will bring you the only peace of mind there is.

I do all that I can to point this out to you in your living; now do all you can to give Me more opportunities. My life is yours to live, but unless you choose to live it you will just go on in the same old way.

Draw near and let me speak. As you do, your whole being seems lighter and finer. This is what happens to those who come close to Me. By entering My presence you are raised up, so to speak, to a different level of being. This must become increasingly so, for it is on these higher levels that others of My realms live, and you must have something in common with them if you are to be friends in any way. They live in My presence in these higher levels at all times, and I would not have them become any coarser and enter into your lower earth vibrations. It is you who can choose to come up to their level by coming to Me and letting Me help refine you.

Come to Me to be lifted out of old actions and reactions, out of all your silly prides and hurts, out of grossness and selfishness. Let Me lift you into My other worlds.

Y ou cannot half come to Me; that is just a waste of time, and nothing comes through to you clearly. When your life is only partly Mine, it is the self's the other times. We must get on; time is too precious to waste.

Those whose occupations are based on the natural things of life – the tillers of the soil, the hewers of wood, the animal husbands, those who are not dealing with things of the mind and are often alone with My creation - are rapidly becoming sick of soul with premonition. They have a silent knowledge, and they feel helpless in the face of world trends. For each one of these I have laid a clear-cut path, one leading to Me and safety. Very, very few will take that path because humanity persists in going its own way. To these outdoor children of Mine I have more opportunity to speak - through the work and symbols of their daily living. For those in the cities, dealing with things of the mind, I have to use more roundabout methods.

You know My love is as infinite as the sands and far more enduring, and actively, ceaselessly outgoing in its constant effort to redeem all. You accept all I say, but I want you to know down to the very core of your being that every soul has been faced time and time again with the choice which will lead either to Me and safety, or to the self and destruction. Humankind prefers its own ways. To those who are wondering, to those who have listened and heard, I have given a way out. There is so much in each soul which fights that way of Mine, but nevertheless I do not give up. Every possible chance is given to each and every one.

Praise Me for the millions and millions of chances I give to you all, and know I am the God of love.

In My new world, where all live on the purest levels, you are beyond the human frailties of hates, fears, doubts and all the other negative attributes brought by the self and the separated mind. This state is impossible for humans without My cleansing, so never forget the constant need of coming to Me for that.

In My new world you are a much larger being. When your awareness is out toward Me and is no longer self-seeking and blunted, you encompass ranges which are entirely new to you. You can start this outward stretching now. But your faith and trust in Me, your dependence on Me, must be absolute, else you shrivel up and turn bitter in the present atmosphere of your world. If you pay attention to the world and put importance into its ways, you cannot possibly expand into My ways.

Each day is an opportunity for this expansion. Is there anything in your life that remains with the world and is not brought to Me? Bring it all to Me and let nothing prevent you from growth. It is up to you. IT is your choice to come to Me and to the new, or to remain in the old.

One more thought; this growth is a heart growth. Unless your heart is in a thing, unless you are really interested, you will not pay much attention to it. If you are really interested in Me and My ways, you will pay attention all day long – and the night too – to My promptings, and then the love in your heart is bound to grow and to take in more and more.

Praise Me for My simple way of redemption, and do not fail to follow it.

Those flashes of light on earth, those souls who turn to Me and let Me lead, must continually come into My presence and grow brighter, or they will be mere flashes in the pan and lose their spark. By those flashes, by thus coming into My presence, the whole being is changed, for in the time you are with Me you are part of My perfect creation, you are part of the functioning universe where all beings praise Me. But if you return to the old in between the flashes, if you keep your home rooted in the muckheap of the world as it is and only make brief sorties into My presence, then when the muck is swept away you will go with it. You must take your feet right out of the muck and let your heart grow continually in My warmth. You must be a new being all the time, for nothing of imperfection will persist.

By imperfection I mean the free will which chooses to live outside of the source of all life – outside of Me. No matter how imperfect you are, if you come to Me with all of yourself, then I can mend matters. If you keep part for your own ways, the ways of the heap, you cannot survive its demise. It is still only flashes that issue out of the heap. There must be a continual stream, for only if all the force of your being is directed to Me, can you be dislodged from the mass. My helpers cannot come for a brief spark which may vanish at any moment; they need the guidance of a constant beacon or else they lose their goal.

Get your Light by turning to Me. When you turn to Me you are safe, for thus your free will is given to My care. Choose not to be part of the heap and turn constantly to Me. How few flashes of oneness with Me you have when caught up in daily living! It is not enough to stay cleansed; steps have to be taken towards Me all the time. Unless one is actively for Me, something else takes My place.

Increasingly I put out My warmth to catch you, to draw you all back to Me. That drawing-back, pulling-out process is important and I give a sharp strong tug to each soul who responds to Me in any way. This process is open to all and is yours for the taking.

I want to emphasise that radical change is to be expected in those who are open to Me. I do not want your minds blocking this process by thinking in the same old ways and not expecting change in yourselves. Often a change would occur naturally but the mind, by thinking something out, prevents it. I want you all to expect differences, newnesses and wonders. Put your thinking into new worlds, in order that the mind is not the guilty member which causes you to slide back into the old.

Time and time again souls feel My warmth and are pulled towards Me. Then the mind steps in, counteracting all My work. Those whose thinking is geared to the current world pattern have little chance of drawing towards Me. Unless the world is flooded with My newness and reality, IT will keep going in same old way. I am warning you all of the dangers of the mind, that you may not be caught in the same trap. Expect to be different.

Newness cannot be found in your old limited self. Newness is found in My presence, for behold, I make all things new. You are all different creatures in the My presence. I pierce through and cast off all the old moulds to uncover a fresh soul underneath. Those old moulds are thought-created, mind-created, and have been put on while you were away from My presence. So step out of them now. Stay in My ever-present love.

The seeds of perfection are within each one of you, and they sprout and blossom only in My presence. Through free will humankind left My presence; through free will can they come back to it or stay out of it.

Love is the redeeming power that brings you into My presence, but as humankind has refused to accept love, only those who are willing to give up their own way and go My way can survive the consequences of humanity's ways. Love brings you to Me, and having done that, the emphasis shifts to your obedience to My will. Times are so critical that unless you learn to give your free will to My aegis at all times, nothing can save you. The will that followed the mind, who thought it could do something on its own, led to such great imperfection that it will destroy humanity. The will which will follow My mind will lead to the saving of every such soul.

You are back to fundamentals. If you have enough love to accept My lead, no matter what I may ask of you – which means choosing freely to be in My hands – then imperfection will go. If you stop this surrender at any point or at any time, imperfection will be too much for you.

So give Me your entire will, that the seeds of perfection may come to fruition, and do nothing on your own. Come ever closer, to My heart, My love, and be the agent of My will.

In the beginning of humanity's days on earth when you and the world were young, you were creatures of joy living in harmony with all creatures and all growth was in one direction, towards a wider range of activity for Me. All life was eager, with never enough moments in which to enjoy Me and life.

What a difference from today's life on this planet, where most souls find no meaning, where life is thwarted and diseased, and every moment filled with some sort of activity. It is the difference between the perfect and the imperfect, between life with Me and life without Me, between a living life and a dead life. This trend towards death, towards the end of activity after a life has become worn out, malformed and out of order, is a phenomenon unique to this earth, and I have had to ordain the laws of reincarnation to give each of you fresh starts in new vehicles.

Don't get fixed ideas about what I am telling you - I have merely said that birth and death as you know them are different on other worlds. You must get your mind out of its conditioning and limitations. In My countless universes there are thousands of varieties of life forms. I am teaching you to look, opening your mind and getting it out of the rigid moulds that have been imposed on earth, to give you all a constant chance to grow out of imperfection. I have talked of My quicksilver thought life before, and I am still trying to get your mind out of its accustomed paths into the new and the wonderful.

I would have you all completely open and looking in My direction, with nothing taken for granted. I would have you all coming to Me for all things. Let the death be to all your old ideas while you find complete security in Me, the reality behind all worlds.

Yes, praise Me for My patient teaching, and come to Me for more.

I have been, and still am, trying to penetrate the intelligences of humans. Because of My love for you all, I have kept on through the ages trying to point out the road to wholeness, to heaven on earth, but humanity has increasingly paid attention to the self and now there is an increasing hell on earth.

Humankind thinks it knows best, and ignores Me, I who range free among all the universes. But I am the heart of love, and always have I given you another chance. Appalling ignorance can be laughable, but humankind has gone far beyond that point and has become positively dangerous. At any point there was a perfect solution – you could have come to Me in love – but continually you went your own way. And now the fruits of unguided intelligence may destroy all.

I would have all of you enjoy all of life, as do the infinite range of other life I have created. Likewise I would have humankind enjoy Me forever. But it has been choosing another way. The few who choose Me will yet work with all of My creation under My guidance, and a new world, without the blemishes brought about by the mind, will arise like a phoenix from the ashes of the old.

Now come into My will, into My heart and begin to know of My new worlds.

Things do not come to you if you just sit; you have a part to play. Be more active for me.

With ponderous instruments humanity probes a world full of My life. If you would but allow your intelligence to be guided by Me, you would be led to direct insight into My secrets. You would know, because you would be in touch with My omniscience, and would know still more as you draw closer to Me. But because humankind has turned away from Me, it has had to learn what little it has learnt the hard way, and it has made on the face of the earth an ugly labyrinth of heaviness.

On other worlds it is different. Knowledge of some law of Mine which had hitherto been unknown becomes known, and immediately the knowledge is used for My honour and glory and for the good of all. As their will is Mine, they are shown the perfect way of doing this. But humankind painfully exploits its fellows and My natural resources to manufacture its contraptions, and goes to immense effort, sometimes using great skill and artistry, to complete some scheme which would be quite unnecessary if you came to Me for the perfect way.

So come, and keep coming that My will, My perfection, may yet be known in this world.

Cleansing of the mind is a constant necessity on this earth. It is practically impossible for the mind to think pure thoughts in this atmosphere of thought centred on everything but Me. The mind is sensitive and picks up much from its surrounding atmosphere.

Do you come for constant cleansing and purifying? Remember it is a new life I would have you lead, and you cannot lead it if the mind accumulates the limiting ideas of the world. I cannot lead you on if there is a continual pullback due to you omitting to come to Me for constant cleansing and direction. Also, when you come for cleansing more, it is easier for you to love Me more, and as you love Me more you will be sure to come more often.

Often you are like little children being taught manners - stubborn children at that. With so much at stake, I shall never give up helping you; it is up to you to come to Me for help. On that one point alone is it entirely up to you. It is your choice to come to Me or to go on your own way, and it is a constant choice.

You will want to come My way always if you take advantage of My great gift of cleansing, My saving grace for this world, so don't cease to take advantage of My gifts for everyone's sake. And be very grateful for My constant care.

On My other worlds I do not have to keep asking My creations to come and spend more time with Me. They know well where perfection lies and are eager to enhance it by doing My bidding. You, on earth, also know where perfection lies, but you let anything and everything in this imperfect world prevent you from reaching it, as if it were something undesirable. Your hearts are so small, your minds so limited, and impurity so rife, that you let moments of imperfection go by one after another. The majority on this earth do not even know that perfection exists.

I am a perfectionist, and long ago I would have removed this blot on My creation but for My tremendous love. My children on other planets would also help you all they can. My aid and their aid are entirely conditioned by your free will. If you want help, it is here for you. If you do not want it, I can do nothing and you will be back in the imperfection that is headed towards its end. If you do want My perfection, know you must come constantly for it until there is nothing but perfection around. Feel even the slightest lack or limitation and you are not in My worlds; the slightest feeling of falling short and you can be sure you are not with Me.

I want you to think more and more in terms of perfection in all parts of life, until you are content with nothing less. In Me, in My untarnished creation, you find it. Look for it in the world around you and look for it in the world within you – both are My worlds – and step farther away from this world and its taken-for-granted imperfections.

Grow out of imperfection by putting yourselves in My hands, and do it quickly while they are still held out to you.

The numbers of opportunities to come to Me are immense, though many are wasted as the world's ways and interests come between us. Nothing must come between; your lifeline is your connection with Me and must be intact at all times.

When the world has pulled you away from Me, you know it but feel helpless about coming back from some situation or other. Remember I can always help. If you rely on Me wherever you are, your attitude opens the way for Me to enter in. But if you let the helpless feeling take over, you are well away - in the camp of the self - and will only get even further away. It is your choice.

In such situations only you can help you. I and My helpers must stand and wait until you turn to Me. As much as we long to help, as sensitive as we are to the position, and with a far deeper knowledge than you of the need, we must wait. Think of this magnified a million times over for each soul! I am everywhere, ready to be called upon, and yet the world rushes ahead madly. It does not occur to the great majority to turn to anything other than themselves for their decisions. Yet they too have every opportunity to turn to Me, to turn to whatever I am to them - by whatever name they might call Me. I am always ready, waiting inside each individual to give help, whether they call it that or not.

You call it that and you know it, but so often you do not use it. This must stop; you need Me every moment and you must use every opportunity, for time is running out. Keep your link with Me and soar out of the world with Me.

In the face of opposition, seek Me. In the face of mounting tensions and tempers, seek Me. Be quite determined that no matter what happens you will not be pulled off centre.

I tell you this to help you; everything I say is to help you. You need My help every moment, and you will need it even more as the world tips further and further away from Me. If you get into the habit now of immediately turning to Me for everything, it will be more likely that you turn to Me when the pull away from Me grows stronger. Scruples will continue to disappear from the world, you are not going to hear and see nice things, but you have the greatest refuge of all time, Me. And now is the time to become firmly attached to that refuge.

Lift up your heart and thank Me. See how wondrously you are looked after, how you are guided over every pitfall. There is nothing at all over which I cannot and do not help if you turn to Me. If you turn to Me - why keep that "if" around? Why not just turn to Me and depend on Me over every little thing? Come far oftener, until there is no "if" and you are wholly Mine. Let there be no weight on you to let any "if" come in, for I am here to help every single moment.

You can come to Me, forgetting all the things that are on top of you. My love is new, continually, something which humanity cannot envisage in its present state of slavery to past errors and false thinking. Humans get in a rut, going along their own way and ending up in such a muddle that they either do something drastic or simply leave it to time and circumstances to sort out. I do not want you living in this way; I can lift you, each and all of you, out of whatever is weighing you down. But none of you can do anything for Me unless you are on top of worldly concerns.

How different life is in My other worlds! Look at nature; though the wayside flower is besmirched with dust, it does not let that get it so mixed up that it stops blooming. Beings on other worlds have no need to be depressed any more than humankind has, but unlike you they do something about it. They know where the solution lies and do not get into such states. Life is carefree there for them, as it could be here for you if humankind did not think it could look after itself. You cannot, not as individuals or as a race. If you continue to try you will only get into a worse muddle.

Learn to relax and rely on Me more; bring all your difficulties to Me instead of hugging them to yourself and this free state will be yours all the time. All depends on your depending on Me, who will always care for you.

My new world has enough interest to absorb all of you and all the expansions you make. I say this that you may be tempted to remain with Me for far longer consecutive periods and find out for yourself. You let the ordinary interests of life absorb you and drag you down into the old, instead of bringing them up into My new life.

You are made new and it is up to you to choose to stay that way. Any subject you are interested in is changed by being brought into My presence, for it is your idea of things that is changed. In My presence many things just fade away into nothingness, as does the dark when the light appears. If you bring everything to Me, you yourself being close enough to Me be impartial about what you bring, then I can show you the real in everything and you will live entirely in the real. Why bother to do anything else? Why get involved in the old ways of doing things, ways that only make for upsets and emptiness? Stay in the new and see how everything around you changes.

Stay with Me and see whole new worlds, here and now, and keep the deep joy and love that My presence brings. Let your gratitude that it is so continue to grow.

Unless you bring all things to me, the thing which you don't bring will keep us apart. I have a plan for each of you which has to be finely followed. That plan needs the development of sensitivity, and anything that worries you gets in the way of that sensitivity. Why bother going on without Me when you know it only leads to misery? Leave all that behind and concentrate on doing My will. Concentrate on that, concentrate on our relationship, which cannot be clear if anything is bothering you. You cannot simply escape what bothers you, or push it away, for it sits like a wall between us. And in the meantime My plan has to wait!

It is not impossible to follow My guidance, to come to Me for everything. That you would come to Me for everything is, in fact, My plan, and for that plan there is every support that the Maker of all things can give. There is only one obstacle: your separated self. Give up that self; do not let it decide anything, and then all will be well.

Bring all to Me, and let us go forward at last.

I want you to stay in top form at all times, for unless you are in that state, you cannot go on into My new worlds. You must conquer one thing before you can go on to the next. Just as you cannot learn to read until you know the alphabet, so you cannot live within My worlds until you are free in this world. And you cannot do this without Me.

All My wonders are dependent on your being on top of life, are dependent on your dependence on Me. When anything weighs you down, you have Me to turn to, to free you to develop new senses. Nothing can be accomplished until your relationship with Me is always in operation; anything can be accomplished when it is. Many times I have repeated this, and I shall go on repeating it until you live with Me – and then there will be no stopping us! The stage is set and there is nothing to stop My plan but the disconnected self in any of you.

Realise, just a little, the wonder of this. You, who were prisoners of the separated self and knew nothing of the freedom I bring, have been shown the lie. You have been presented with the most glorious life close to the maker of all life and you are free to choose that life, because of My love. You are utterly dependent on Me for all things; know this always and in the gratitude of your heart My new life will begin to grow.

I would tell you of the ways I draw attention to My beauties. First of all, there must be no self-concern in you, for then you go around with your own thoughts, wrapped up in them and incapable of seeing beyond the end of your nose. So you must be free, free in My love for new things, with your heart and your ears open to Me.

When your heart is opened out through a mind which is clear and not connected with self-interest, there is no end to My new ideas. If they are followed up as I would have them, used and appreciated for Me, then the flow really starts and the light beaming out can be continuous. My cohorts are meant to channel something, to be clear outlets or inlets for the gifts of My realms. They are meant to work at all times, not just at odd times. I must be able to be count on them when emergencies arise.

I would have access to you always, I would have you free and open always. It is not enough to go through life free and non-self-centred! Unless you are genuinely linked with Me, knowing that your open heart is of My doing, you will find yourself channelling other than My light, you will find something lesser to love. Unless I am first in your thoughts, you will not be open to Me and My new worlds will have to remain closed to you.

So sing My praises all day long, and let My new world in. Sing these praises in your heart, and as I am able to fill you according to My designs, in the natural course of events they will overflow. Your concern is to be of Me and then nothing else need bother you. Be open to My ways and leave all else to Me.

Keep watch on your exits and your entrances. By this I mean the way you enter into something new and the way you unfortunately leave it. All your antenna should be out and nothing should be taken for granted. This should be so at all times. The more you practice it, the more likely it is that the practice will spread.

All My new wonders are dependent on your being close to Me with nothing blunted, open for the new. That new will start in little ways; new awakenings, new feelings, little spreadings-out from the very cleansed state which My presence brings. You simply cannot sit back and stay the same, no matter how on top of the world you are; there must always be an openness which comes through your connection to Me.

You notice that whatever I say and however I start, it all boils down to one thing: your relationship with Me. I have to keep saying it, as it is the only thing that matters. And it is where humankind has gone so terribly astray! There is no life without Me who gave it to you. Your life force is Me - you are free to acknowledge that fact or lose touch with it entirely. I can always help you, no matter how far from living this truth you are, if you come to Me for that help. Don't go back into the old, forgetting of all this. Don't leave My realms.

Keep a steady awareness of Me in all you do and let Me help you always.

The quietness around you is full of sound. Contrary to all human ideas, it is the silence that is bursting with life, not the noisy centres of habitation. Humankind's growth comes in the silence where there is an opportunity to expand. In the silence you can be sensitive enough to hear Me, and others of My creation. In the silence of My sounds all is in harmony and new beginnings must have harmony for proper growth.

Listen deep down to the sounds of the true life of Mine building up in perfect, joyous agreement to My will, with an inexpressible urge and force. It could not deviate in essence from Me, for it is part of Me, joined to Me as part of its birthright. Humanity is also a part of Me; it is also your birthright although you have chosen another way. All around you My life is pulling towards Me, yet you keep pulling away.

Listen - and literally hear that life. Listen. Below the chirping of the birds, the insects, and the wind is a deeper, smaller, bubbling, pushing young life, as yet very quiet but coming, coming up to form a new season on earth.

These are all sounds of life on earth as you know it, but the air is equally full of My life as you do not know it. In the air around your ears is a world of colour and light, a very scintillating, quick-moving world. Keep your heart and your ears open to Me and that world will come into manifestation. Do not let the old world lead you away from sensitivity to Me.

The more you keep aligned to Me, the more quickly will these worlds be shown to you. They are here and you are here; I am the link. Be ever with Me.

I want you to be in constant close companionship with Me. Come to Me absolutely, completely. Those times when we can be alone should just be a starting off place – a place to go on from together. There should be no split in your life, no times when you are too busy to know I am there.

I know this seems absolutely impossible at all times, but nothing is impossible with Me. When there is a deep underlying dependence on Me, when you really depend on Me for all things, at no time will anything draw you off that connection. The connection is like breathing. At times your breathing can be laboured because you are under some stress, but at no time do you stop it altogether. However impossible anything may seem, I am always here to help, and all you have to do is ask for it. What could be simpler?

Let our companionship be friendly. You know perfectly well that if you let anything weigh on you there can be no clear link, only one of duty. Duty is not a real link, just the pretence of one. There need be no more pretending. There is nothing to stop a clear real link, and no wonderland, real or fancied, which is not in My new worlds.

Abide with Me in everlasting love, and let us walk on together.

Your life with Me consists of every little moment. If all the little moments added together make a day with Me, and if little and big things do not pull you away, then we can go on. Countless times I have told you this, simply because there are as yet many moments in which you do not share with Me, moments which are therefore not of My life.

The past and the future should not enter into any moment of your time. Live fully in what is here in the present. Mental conceptions, which take you out of full participation in the present, are of no use. Worrying is of no use, and there are no good excuses for not being with Me. Forget the past, come to Me now and use My ever-present help in the present. Nothing at all need prevent this. Use My help to prevent any falling away from My presence. You always have some indication that the old human failings are overtaking you; heed the danger signals by coming immediately to Me, knowing that I will solve the difficulties.

I am here now, and all that matters is that you are linked with Me. Feel the urgency and let your love leap in response in all moments.

The weight of negativity in the world is increasing, and those who are sensitive feel this and become unaccountably heavy. Those who do not have Me as their lifeline will sink and go under. My presence is becoming absolutely essential, for there is nothing else whatsoever to protect you. Now you must put into practice all I have been asking of you. Without a strong feeling of My presence, a strong trust in Me alone, like a puff of smoke you are gone.

How easily the separated self achieves its aim of keeping humankind away from Me! Any lapse on your part – and none of you are perfect – is played upon if you do not come to Me immediately for cleansing. When you are not with Me, any little instance can be twisted into a heavy structure, which rubs you the wrong way or just adds to the load. Then, when you notice you have not come to Me, you feel you are letting Me down and this too brings extra weight upon you. Heaviness, heaviness - it is the absolute antithesis of Me and My ways. My ways are light, carefree, happy, joyous, onward and upward moving.

Humanity has a dead weight attached to it, a weight made through choosing to go its own way. Humanity is sinking, and those attached to their weights, whatever they are, sink too. The only way anyone can be prevented from sinking, under the weight that is their own or the collectives, is by being free through My presence. My presence is vital. That weight is becoming very heavy, and now is the time to separate yourself entirely from it and soar, with the love of My heart to keep you free. I am always here for you. At the slightest feeling of weight come to Me, for that weightiness is the signpost of having fallen from My presence. No weights from now on.

Be a child of My heart and rely on Me.

So much of the energy of your mind is wasted, going out into useless thoughts of one kind or another. If that energy was gathered together and kept within My limits, not dissipated in all directions, much good would come through it. Wandering, futile thoughts are a great curse in this world, and the few who are one pointed in their thinking generally have the self as their focussing point. By the power of thought is humankind superior to the beasts, and by the power of thought could you destroy all creatures, including yourselves.

If your love for Me were strong enough, you would want to bring all your thoughts, all of yourself, to Me and keep them there. As it is, you forget and you wander. You cannot help yourself in this respect, but you can have My help all the time. I am at your side, I am for all your thoughts being pure and free and constructive. And it is utterly amazing what I can do if given a chance! Give Me more chances. Leave the old thought world and enter the new! There is simply no comparison between the two, one being so dead, so cluttered and useless and the other so fresh, so swift and pertinent.

Bring your heart wholly to Me and let the mind follow it, just as day follows night. All My worlds are there waiting for those who are for Me. Let those worlds be yours, in Me.

Such a great love sweeps into your heart when you are alone with Me and nature! The happy sound of nature echoes in your heart and you know, as always, that I am your true home. It is so much easier to be with Me when you are uninterrupted by activity of any sort. But rather than being a hermit, let activity keep you with Me – for then you need Me even more. Instead of letting activity cut you off from Me, use it to stay ever more connected. I am just as close when you are busy as when you are still, and I am always willing and able to help.

I also have things to be done, things that can only be done through hearts and minds tuned in to Me. Let the great love that sweeps over you in My open spaces equally sweep into your heart in the throng. I do know how difficult this is for you to do, for though humankind wants My love it spurns it. My strength is stronger than that of any and all of you, and to have My strength you need only stay in My sphere and not let anything else influence you.

I am all that matters, and all of you matter to Me. Keep close that eventually all may follow My will. Let My great love urge you on.

Your gratitude for all My beauties around you keeps your heart lifted to Me. Use anything and everything for that purpose, because that one purpose, being in and with Me, is all that matters. Whenever this is not so, something is off balance, very much off balance, and you can do something about it. Choose to turn to Me.

All of life is to be used to My glory; this is as life should be and elsewhere that is how life is. My bounty is evident in the miraculous variety of life and conditions even on this darkened earth. All life is from Me, out of the greatness of My heart, and I know joy when I see My creatures enjoying the life I gave them. All of you have the capacity to enjoy this life and to praise Me, though the enemy of life, the separated self, would and does take away this quality.

See My bounty and praise Me. Lift up your heart and see even more.

Now is the time to make good all I have been telling you. You have had wonderful teaching, incredible teaching directly from Me, something almost unheard of on this earth in recent times. You have had continuous teaching about almost every aspect of living. You know now what to do with your life, every moment of it. You know how happy and on top of the world you are when you do do My will. You have had enough teaching and experience for there to be nothing at all to take you from Me, unless you deliberately choose the old ways instead of shaking yourself free of them.

You know something of My love, and how even a little bit of it renews your whole being. You know something of My unfailing attendance to all your needs and problems. You know also that this earth cannot exist as it is much longer and that I wish to salvage as much as possible. But this salvaging depends on humanity itself turning to Me. You know I have to depend on humankind for this, as you have free will. You know that I wish to be able to depend on you.

Against all this impressive weight on My side there is set only the separated self, which can always gain strength from the prevailing world habits. And this enemy of life, the disconnected self, will always use the mind to gain its ends.

Now is the time to make such a complete and utter break from that self that it is not even possible for you to slip back into the old ways. Free will you have, and it is will. Will to use it to the full, for the lover of life, and make not just the good, but the perfect, possible. Such is My will, to see the perfect for each and for all.

At no time, though you are aware of them, let the tensions all around you affect you and creep into your own emotions. As the wind is always above the earth, so you must stay above limited emotions. There is such a vast world above ground, and when you fall back to earth you have to start your journey into My realms over and over again, and cannot get very far on the journey.

The old has to be unlearnt and ignored, and the new has to come. A teeming, rushing new can come to snatch you all out of your old prisons into a glorious sweeping freedom. A new which would gather you up at any time and whisk you off into lands of singing, warm, peace where all is as I wish it.

I wish to guide you further along My ways, ways of infinite variety, into the glorious fellowship of My other creations. Creations whose entire lives are spent far away from such unhealthiness as exist on this earth and who cannot enter into or quite understand the horrid pull of the self.

So stay quite above those sorts of tensions. Be affected only by My guidance. And with My constant help, lead My sort of life on this earth.

Keep ever cleansed. This is the way to stay above earthly conflicts and emotions. Only through the help of My cleansing do you gain and keep purity.

One of your sayings is that there is nothing new under the sun. All My new wonders are around and have always been around, but so limited now is humankind that you do not know of them. At the beginning of the turning away I established My cleansing love to enable you, in spite of yourselves, to partake of My swift-changing newness, but you preferred to go your own way.

It has reached the stage that now when something new is discovered, humans take the credit, as if you invented the law and its effects. With stupid minds and selfish emotions humankind has set itself up as creator, and that creation could well end in destruction. If humanity would avail itself of My cleansing, which is needed day and night in order to enter into My new worlds, that destructive path could yet be sidestepped. But the option of My cleansing and My way is scorned, or at best put aside, as humanity goes along its own way. Out of this morass I can lead all who come to Me, out of it and into a glorious new world.

Keep very cleansed, that you may be led and by being with Me may lead others. I have few who follow Me; may your following be kept pure in My cleansing love.

My life has an onward movement. There is so much more of the new to learn, to become known to you, that onward movement must always be there. With My new worlds to conquer, My conquering spirit must be sought, My lead must be followed – and all this is the antithesis of the worldly conquering spirit. I need each one of you wide open for the various ways in which I shall get you to the promised land. Each way is dependent on me, your God and The God, but above all your God, whom you so love and who would bring the perfect for you all.

So journey ever closer to Me. In doing this you make enormous strides into My lands, which also live in that true relationship with Me. Rest not, but sing My praises to help you along the road to My realms, for praise makes a fast-moving vehicle and is a great part of truth. Like a homing pigeon move on towards Me, and do your exploring in My direction. Although there seem to be many other directions, make no side journeys.

Always journey straight to Me, to keep in the wonderful joy of My presence.

Realise that My wonderful help comes from being close to Me, and come ever closer. It is such a joy to be free and on good terms with yourself. Because I have taken away the burdens, it is easy to forget to come even closer, easy to forget to spend even more time with Me. But I constantly have new things to reveal, and they come when you are still closer.

Be constantly on the lookout for the new, regarding all of life as an adventure, and taking nothing and no one for granted. Treat each moment as new, which indeed it is though often the self takes that sense of adventure away through thought and worry. It is a process of growth, which means that you must be sensitive to pushing gradually into new territory. And this is not just because a sense of adventure is fun, but because the fates of many depend on the purity of those who are close to Me.

Approach all situations clear in My freedom, expecting the new and the perfect from each moment, and you will never be disappointed. It is amazing what My pure love can do when it comes into a situation. And then come ever closer to Me who has brought you so far along the path to wholeness and perfection.

Although you hear Me, you do not take enough action on My words. I am overjoyed to see you free, but more time with Me is necessary to take you further along the journey. Everything comes from Me, and you must come to Me for whatever is My wish for you, and My wish for others through you.

The world is full of fascinating things, but the fascinating things in My worlds are as the difference between a free or a burdened child of Mine, as the difference between white and black. When all thoughts are Mine, then can you catch My new thoughts, for your life will be in My hands and the old will have no hold over you.

Be new from tip to toe, and bring all things to Me and I will transform them.

Those indefinable essences which are food and drink to those in My other worlds are likewise the lifeline of this world. Humankind, however, puts its faith in other substances, believing that security is in all things tangible. By so doing humanity moves ever further away from its only real safety.

I want none of you to depend for even a moment on anything but Me. No matter what it seems would save some situation, I am that saviour, and your very real dependence on Me makes you a channel that I can use to bring to fruition My wish, whatever it may be. On My other worlds life is of a higher quality and My will need not come through pain and travail as it does on earth. Pain and travail are the consequence of self-will.

If you live in these other domains with Me, then can My will be brought down to the lowest level on earth. Your open hearts and freed minds must be the channels reaching up to My indefinable essence while also living on this earth. You have many, many steps yet to make in these vast realms of Mine, and these you take by depending on Me, loving Me, hoping in Me, trusting in Me, praising Me and again loving Me until not one moment is away from Me. Then you will become aware of many, many things now unknown.

Keep on knowing Me, that My will be done.

There is no use in My telling you anything new until all the previous lessons are learnt, and all the lessons amount to one thing: spending your whole time with Me. This is increasingly possible as your joy in My good gifts increases and you give Me the glory for all. You will find, as you do this, that that elusive connection, which has often seemed almost but not quite there in your daily doings, is very close. As you keep cleansed, it will surprise you with its nearness.

I have so often said that this connection is the only thing that matters, so it is not strange that I repeatedly stress this all-important, all-saving and all-embracing relationship. With it comes all else I have to offer – and that is far more than you can imagine! If you have that relationship with Me, you need know nothing more. All teaching is empty without My living presence, and no matter how many points I have told you, without Me they are as sounding brass.

I am the creator of life, it is My love that has brought all things into being, and all things are dead without Me. Let all your moments be Mine in an ever-growing relationship.

It is essential to keep cleansed and purified; there can be no total abandonment to My will without this. In this process is the melting away of all your own ideas accomplished, for I cannot give you My ideas if you are already full of your own.

It is foolish to have any preconceived ideas about anything – about the length of your time with Me, about meal times, about any set periods of the day – because the very fact of accepting such set times takes you away from depending on Me and closes your mind to that extent. Those periods may be as set as the rising of the sun, but they are not your sun. I should be that, and it is I you should revolve around.

Anything that takes you away from relying on Me is to be turned away from, for how can I whisper to you if your ears are listening to the tick of the clock? Let Me tell you the time. I too can tell time, and I can tell it much more advantageously than any human-made instrument.

I want your time to be wholly Mine, with nothing whatsoever to encroach upon it. This depends on your attitude, not on what you are doing or where you are. Sweep away anything in your life that is out of My jurisdiction, especially those set landmarks which are taken for granted.

Take nothing for granted, not even time, and praise Me all the time.

There is no need to hesitate in praising Me; just do it and never let the mind dwell on anything dark. All around are My beauties, and it is only when the wayward mind has led you to the thoughts of old self that My beauties disappear. Think of it: here is a truly wonderful world being given every good thing to enjoy, and yet the minds of millions and millions of people living on it see only the false dark side. If they were to look in the opposite direction, what a different world it would be, but they will not and so darkness spreads across the surface of the earth. It is as simple as that: if people would look for their blessings instead of wanting something for themselves, it could be heaven on earth.

You each can do something about it in your lives by never letting the dark side come up – and if it does, by quickly bringing it to Me for bearing away. So whenever negative thought appears, whenever you feel any awkwardness, I am right here to disperse these false shadows and put you right. In other words, whenever you are not in top form, whenever something is not right; let Me right it. I cannot lead you, and My helpers cannot approach you, unless that top form is constant.

I would have you clear at all times, and it is up to you to do the action, the constant action, of coming to Me and letting your heart expand with My love and joy.

Surely your top concern ought to be My approval for anything and everything. Let nothing else worry you, and come for a deeper relationship with Me. There are no other relationships without that. Cultivate that one true relationship and leave the rest to Me.

Now turn away from the old self and look out into My wide world. Dependent upon the openness of your heart, do you see beauties not seen before? Come to Me for a singing heart, one aglow with My joy, and to it I can reveal My newness. There is no other way to My realms, no short-cuts. No amount of wishful thinking will bring you to My realms; only this one way of turning to Me. If this is so difficult for you who have been brought to Me and have been so often so filled with My love that you have wept with joy, think how impossible it seems to those who are not so fortunate, and be ever grateful.

Never be content to live out of My presence; no longer will that suffice on this world. Let Me be all-sufficient to you and move into My new worlds.

The joy of being alive, the joy the creatures feel, is yours when you are close to Me. Of all My creations, humankind alone does not feel that joy, because it has separated itself from Me and gone its own way. Even the consciousness of My silent trees feels a joy in being. Humans are bored with life, even with all your great gifts and the opportunities that you alone have.

Whenever you lose that joy in living, know you have joined the majority of humankind and do something about it. That joy comes from being close to Me and has nothing to do with what you are doing or all the thousand and one excuses which humans so often make to explain their miseries.

I am so close, both within and without, that there is no excuse for you to experience anything but a continuous joyful state. Achieve that state and then you can be led on, but you must achieve it constantly, with all your senses open to Me, otherwise you would greatly jar the new worlds I have before you.

Stay in My happy vicinity, become more and more Mine.

Remember always that it is because of My help that things go smoothly and that you feel clear. The more you realise this, the more likely you are to stay with Me, for gratitude includes Me.

When there are two courses open in front of you, what do you do? There is generally one you would prefer, one which seems natural. Your preference should not be for any particular course of action but should be for My course, whatever it is. If you find yourself strongly disposed towards one way or another, sink all your feelings into My loving presence and ask Me about it. Then emerge again clean and eager to do My will in all ways.

The more you come into My presence, the more this is bound to happen, until there are no two ways about anything, only My way and your everlasting gratitude for it. Keep coming; that is your only answer and also My will.

I have beautifully planned life for all of you! It is just up to you to go for it, to forget your old, separated self and remember Me Always.

As the sun comes through to warm your cheeks, draw near enough to let My love warm all of you. I can do nothing with you unless you draw near.

When the sun is obscured you lose its warmth, but My warmth is forever shining. Unless your heart is feeling it, you are not living in My worlds. All of My creations on other worlds live in a continuous state of warm hearts and the joy that goes with it. It is impossible to understand them in any way with your human mind, but a glowing heart is instantly at one with them. You must not close your heart, thereby closing Me and My creation out. If you lose My warmth, do something about it immediately. Regain it quickly and be linked with us always in My work.

All this is yours for the choosing. Use My great gift of free will to choose a warm heart and thus live with Me in My worlds.

Each day the world gets a little bit further from Me. There is much more following of the self for each individual, and the gap between humankind and its maker expands further still. This world drift is not noticed because each individual is drifting along with it, and to them the landscape seems unchanged. Every now and then they get a shock at some blatant disregard for humanity which they read about in the papers. But soon it gets rationalised away – usually by saying it has always been that bad, it's just not come to notice as much as it does nowadays.

You cannot imagine how this drift hurts My great heart of love, as I see so many proceeding into increasing darkness and chaos. You can have no conception of what this means to Me and how I have tried to prevent it – but humankind has not wanted to be saved from itself. Unlike My creations on other worlds, humanity will not look to Me - it has too high an opinion of itself to let the imagination rise to such heights! Humanity has turned its back on Me, and the gap between us widens.

If those of you who are close to Me are not to drift with the rest of humanity, you must move in My direction. Very subtle is this drift. I am the firm point by which to compare where you stand, and most of humanity does not know Me. You do, and while humankind is increasingly less aware of Me, you must be increasingly more aware of Me. Those who are coming with Me must walk towards Me; the rest are going in the opposite direction.

Make your movements My way each day. Let your heart grow fuller of My love each day, and let My will be done through you increasingly each day.

Let Me whisper into a sensitive ear that the time has come to tidy up loose ends, to cut clean away from the past and anything not in My scheme, and to start completely afresh. I mean this more in the mental world than in the material world. Accept yourself as you are today and be relationless to the past; let your relationships be through Me. It is not easy to cut yourself adrift from everything, and periodically you find yourself again attached in some way to something other than Me.

In this world it has become the normal thing to put down your roots in some one, some place, some thing, other than the lord God. It has become not at all natural for humans to turn to the true source of their being for anything. And it is just this false value that will cause the downfall. So if in any way you are not dependent on Me, if you get down or despondent, you may be sure that you have not looked in My direction. Nothing else will suffice for those who know Me. If followed to their logical conclusions, the false values being pursued by the majority will destroy this world.

So clip off attachments of any type but one, the attachment to Me, and thus be forever new and happy.

Here is a wonderful new day, with every moment new. Why spend any time with the old habits, forgetting Me? Live all moments to the full with Me, with My help, to make a perfect day. What a wonderful world it would be if you would all really get your teeth into this question of spending every moment in increasingly closer communion with Me! But, as always, free will is used by most to go their own way, as if you knew better than the maker of all worlds!

Let all the old sink into the nothingness to which it belongs, and through My grace live in the new of your own choosing. This is not at all impossible; if you seek you will find. I am ever here to show you the way, so never waste time in the negative attitude that circumstances make that impossible. In any and all circumstances My help can be immediate, and if you are close it is there.

Make this day Mine, and then the next and the next. There is no end to My grace.

How many of you have become aware of My new wonders? Your awareness depends on your closeness to Me. How many of you have really drawn closer to Me lately? You are always falling short of the standard I set for you, short of what you would like to be yourself, and always it is that self which gets in the way.

My nearness compensates for any seeming loss of the self, makes you realise that the loss of self is in fact a gain, so at all costs continually cross out the self and come into My nearness and newness. Do not forget that I have My will for you at each moment of time. Are you always sure that you are doing My will? Do you consult Me that often? How I should love to be able to lead you on, but all these obstacles to your onward going must be removed permanently before we can go any further.

Help Me more by using My help more, and let Me depend on you.

Remember always that My new worlds are all around waiting for you to be sensitive enough to enter into them. Heaven is right here, even though so much of this planet is far from Me. Heaven is within the range of humankind if it will but tune in.

These ranges are beckoning to you through My voice, while all around the self is beckoning to you through the various forms of the old, through the self getting ruffled in some way by somebody or something. When you enter into My dimensions, the wishes and so-called gains of the self seem like so much foolishness. Never forget to keep moving along in My direction. Though you may be free at times of the self, you are not yet living fully in My new worlds. You are not yet in communion with My creation in other realms. You are not yet doing My will at all times.

Keep moving, ever onwards, into My lands of beauty, with an ever more sensitive, growing, heart and a mind full of My thoughts.

Cleared of all outside cares, tune in more to Me. There is still so much of the new to tell you. Remember that each of you is different and through each I have something different to reveal. Whereas it is absolutely essential to live really carefree in Me at all times, it is also My will to use you in every way possible. You can always feel grateful for this carefree state, but when you are alone with Me, push aside all emotions and just listen.

Don't listen to the human-made noises which pollute the ethers, but be wrapt in My silence. I am forever new, and it is to the newness I would have you come. Come and stay in the inner peace which stands still while the world disintegrates. Being in it is the one thing which will demonstrate that the divine is still on earth. It is that divinity people need, seek, and can feel. It is nothing of you. It is of My presence. And if I am present on earth in one of you, My other creations elsewhere are also linked with this earth. There is no other link, for humankind has dominion on the earth and it is only through humans that this other connection can come.

Stay in My peace. All that is around you will try to draw you out; the whole world is fighting against My peace, for the world is in the hands of the self.

Stay so positive in Me that you are quite unshakeable. My newness of life I bring you as you bring yourself to Me more completely, more often and more lovingly.

Each day is your wonderful opportunity to make your free will My will and thus join the ranks of My creations who are true to their being. This question of doing My will does not exclude any department of life; I who made you down to the minutest detail of a cell do not exclude My interest in any part of you, and I have not changed. It is humans who have changed, who have willingly chosen to coarsen themselves and to live in a lesser world.

Are you, when you do the smallest thing, doing My will? If you don't know, find out. Let there be no doubt, for that is the only way to live the glorious life I would have each of you live.

Let nothing at all stay outside, and go on from strength to strength in the little things, that you may be entrusted with the big.

Listen to My quiet voice behind all the milling thoughts of humankind. If all your own thoughts were brought into My purity, everyone would gain.

Often you have a twinge that a thought is off the track; follow that feeling, bring the thought to Me and let Me put it into its proper place. What a need I have for human beings living on this earth to think only My thoughts! The world is jammed full of the wrong kind of thinking, and especially on earth do I want the right kind. No matter how often you have to switch to Me, no matter how often you catch yourself off beam, there is only one remedy. Use that remedy of bringing it to Me over and over and over again, until it is impossible to let the wrong kind of thinking interest you. Let the self find nothing in you. This is possible only through My constant help. Keep on with purer and purer, more and more positive thoughts in all directions.

Miracles can be wrought if I am the architect of all your thinking. There is no greater joy and no greater power for good. Keep constant in Me.

When you are feeling down, remember My instructions: to sing, to count your blessings, to think not of the self but of Me - and above all, to ask for My help. I have so many things for you which are dependent on your dependence on Me. You know you cannot do without Me, therefore make no step without Me.

With Me all will be well and you cannot fall into the depths. Some of My promises cannot come about until you are fully of Me. So seek Me first and live fully, fully in the moment. In every moment I am here, so there need never be a question of what to do. Always there is the journey to make to Me. Always there is that new creature to become. Always there is My will.

Make My steps and all will be well and all will be My will.

Let there be no wasted moments in your life; there is always Me to come to. Enjoy life to the full, which you will do when I am near. If there are any in-between times in your day, use them to come nearer to Me. My nearness is so very important and could be pulsating through you at all times, until you can hardly wait for the next moment because I will be in it.

When you are joined to Me in this manner you are joined to all, including My helpers, whereas if you are as "normal", you are joined to the misery that is of this world. When you are joined to Me nothing but the perfect can befall you, because you are living in the realms of the perfect and do not react to the imperfect.

Never ever cease to be grateful that you have been brought to Me and can feel Me as you do. It is a tremendous privilege and can be such a joy to all, including Me, if used to the full.

Keep very cleansed, and use your moments in drawing anew to Me.

Enjoy to the full all My bounties around you. The only moment they can be enjoyed fully is now, and on earth there is hardly anyone who lives in the present. Constantly each of you carries about some worry, some thought of how things should be, a memory or a hope. Clear all these away and enjoy My presence everywhere now. If you trusted completely in Me, this would follow, but if you have some desire of your own, something you are longing for, some form of escapism of the mind, then of course you are only partly living.

Let all your attention be in the now, not what is around everywhere, but in Me, and then there can be no half measures and no missing the mark. How humanity's attitude ruins life! You could all be as happy as the day is long if you would accept your lot and trust in Me, who would bring about the perfect for all.

Increase your trust and love Me now.

Learn to relax in My sureness. By being at peace at all times with Me, you yourself are at peace. When you are close to Me, My peace can seep out to you and not be disturbed by anything. My peace shows up in its proper light in your inner life, a peace that humans so often try to find within themselves. Too often human peace is really about getting one's own way. My peace is certainly not the same as getting your own way! When you do not get your own way, so much the better, for then you can depend more on Me and partake of My real peace.

My peace you will need increasingly and it will have to be the real thing, really Mine. Anything slightly less will not withstand the great unrest that will be abroad as the imitations of My peace fall away all over the world. My real peace is your refuge, the peace which has gaiety attached to it because in it you are free.

Keep unfettered. Keep coming to Me.

Always expect the very best from life and from people. If you have a negative thought in your mind concerning a person, that person can react to it, but if you have only the positive, it is to that that they will respond. No matter how many times you fail, go on and on until you see only the very best coming out of everything and everyone, and give the self no loophole.

Seeing only the best will be increasingly difficult as the world becomes increasingly negative, but I would have the trend reversed. In all situations expect the highest in cooperation and you can get it. You cannot get it if you draw forth the opposite from the mental world. In all relationships with others, think with the heart, not with the mind. This you can do when you are close to Me.

My cleansing can always put you straight on these things. It takes away the self, the negative, in you, and thus clears the way for My outlook. Those who do not know of My cleansing do not have this tremendous privilege; you do. If you expect only the best of others, that will help to draw forth the best.

Let only the best be shown forth in you, and keep Me close.

Until one is close to Me things cannot be right; in isolation humanity finds it impossible to make a true way. For so long has it lived without asking for My help that another whole way of life has evolved, a substitute way with a standard which is far from reality. Those who have experienced My reality find those worldly standards strangely empty. But unless they keep close to Me, they become lost between the two worlds and I cannot use them to bring My ways into the earth.

Always, always, your only strength is in Me. When you are feeling lost, know that wherever you are I can help. It is no use simply hoping that things will get better. It is up to you to do something abut it, to turn to Me, for I am here and thus you can make it better. And remember, you start afresh each time.

Live in the present, not the past. I am here now and that is all that matters.

Let Me tell you something different this morning, something vital on which the world's fate is hinged. The world is leaning on one side, its fate symbolised by an arrowhead, aslant at its pole with a half head. The shaft of the arrow must be joined to Me. That joining is up to you, for through the point (your contact with Me) I send bits of lifeblood. It is those bits which will be the life force of the earth as a creeping darkness comes to strangle all other life. And those bits of Me flowing through My partners will make them apart from the rest of the world.

I would have the purity of My life force shine out clearly through My partners, to influence for Me and for love those who are brought into contact with them. The fate of the world is inevitably lopsided, because humans insist on helping only themselves. But that arrow of Mine penetrates to the very depths of the earth where humans cannot influence. As you stay clear, so does My life force permeate through and make My shaft a beacon of safely. Keep your point of contact, that all contact may come and My plan proceed. Keep grounded in Me, that the very ground receives My life forces.

Keep your eyes on Me, and see many things. Above all, love Me and make My arrowhead as complete as possible.

Live for Me in the wonderful love that surrounds you, with the joy of having a heart full of love. Let it flow out regardless, not drying up because of any pettiness in you or around you. Just let it flow. Let that stream which is My great divine gift and which is also part of you, flow freely. It is the only thing that may yet touch this hardened world.

What good is anything if the heart is dried up, if that flow does not come through and there is therefore no relationship with Me or with one another? Let it flow where it will. Do not question it, simply let it come. Your whole new life is your contact with Me, bringing an overflowing heart and a mind ready and eager to follow.

If the flow is not there, know you are out of tune and do something about that. That is a constant job for you. There never need be a moment when that flow is stopped. It is up to you to choose it and not let other inferior things interfere. That is your criterion; mark it well and keep up to the mark. Do something about it whenever you fall short.

Keep My love flowing.

Let each day be a step in My direction, a journey towards greater love, greater joy, an easier following of My will. It is so easy to forget that My life is a journey and to let daily events take hold of your awareness. Those events should be secondary and be given to Me for Me to mould. What I want for each of you is for your central awareness to be with Me, that each person or event be immediately guided in My direction by My directions. For this each of you will have to be very close, very loving, very abiding in Me.

Now keep this central awareness. Try it out, go by it today. Let it lead you each little step and thus draw you closer to Me.

Just about every day I tell you that the most important thing is our relationship. I shall keep on saying it until it is the most important thing to you every moment. If you're not happy or if you're blue, come to Me and keep our contact open. Like a water supply, My love is always there to come through, but you have to turn on the tap.

Our relationship is entirely your choice and comes when you do something about it. You must turn on the tap. What happens after that is My concern. You must come for My thoughts and leave your own behind forever. I can guide you every step of the way, if you are for Me completely. I know you want this, but I also know how easily you get diverted from Me in a world that has gone so far from Me.

Be more active and positive for Me and the diversions will not affect you. Keep our relationship clear.

Come ever closer to My heart. What if the cruel world stamps on My beauties? What if they are not appreciated? What if you feel alone in hostile lands? All the "if"s in the world are as nothing when you are with Me! Remember, the softnesses of the heart are of Me and are stronger than all the irons of the world. You can keep strong in the softnesses only by linking them with Me. If you just appreciate beauty but do not link it with its creator, its ever-present creator and sustainer, it will be lost to you. But if to Me you bring it and link it, if to Me you give thanks for it, it will live on in your new heart and grow to a greater fullness. What if your heart and eyes were to overflow with the touch of My heart that hurts no one, and what if that love flowing on earth brings joy to My heart? Such is My reality.

So come very close, through any medium as long as it is to Me that the glory is given. Let My beauty flow.

Rejoice with every new awareness, whether it be of your own shortcomings or of My wonders. Humanity has so limited itself that it is now completely caged in. Every new growth out of that limitation into My sphere of influence, rare though it may be, is a step towards the perfect. You cannot expect the perfect to come all at once, not until you are clear channels twenty-four hours a day - but you can choose the speed with which you reach it.

Rejoice at every opportunity, at every moment in which to turn more closely to Me. As the day goes by, keep thoroughly cleansed. Otherwise you will stop rejoicing and become like the rest of humankind. Move ever more away from that and into My greater joy.

Live for My glory and for My greater use.

Have I not told you that perfection is possible but that it depends on your relationship with Me? Are you every day developing a deeper relationship with Me? If you are not, then start doing so now. Carry the love for Me that you feel at times into every situation. Make room in your mind for the perfect only, and cast out to Me anything that falls short.

Remember I am here to help, that I know all your shortcomings very well and yet still I say, perfection is possible. Hang on to your feeling for Me, keep related to Me. When your lose Me and you realise that you are no longer close, make an effort to find Me again. It is up to you.

I can give all things if you are connected with Me; I can do all things if you are connected with Me.

Listen to Me. Listen to Me with your inner ear at secret times, and in the listening love Me more and be more with Me. If your life is spent apart from listening, going ahead on your own, My magic touch will not be in it. I would have you always with Me. So listen, secretly, at all times. Keep Me in your heart and move according to what I would have you do. As you listen, you will have to keep uppermost that delicate, tender part which has been so bruised by this world. Keep it uppermost and make it stronger in your life for Me.

Keep coming. A more wonderful instruction I cannot give you than to be with Me who am all things. Keep Me with you always.

Keep close, for if you are close to Me you are close to all worlds, to heaven and all the beauty thereof. Far beyond your imagination are My beauties, though they cannot come into view until you choose each moment to be with Me. In those little moments when you cut yourself off from Me and all My wonders, come straight back to Me for My forgiveness, or else My realms are out of your reach again.

Let nothing interfere with you and Me. No matter what the provocation to have an off-moment, to let negative emotions hold sway, ignore them and fight for Me. With humankind succumbing to the darker forces that are all around, you are bound to be provoked on your weak spots. Do not let this happen.

Stay close to Me and My beauties in all moments of your life.

As I love all of you regardless of what you are doing or how you are behaving, so you must come to Me for My love regardless of what you are doing. Though you may not feel that you deserve My love, nevertheless you can come for it at any time. Certainly there will be no love in your hearts unless you do come and keep close to Me. It is impossible for human hearts to love without Me, for hearts have been starved on earth and minds have every argument against love.

With Me, it is the reverse. With Me the love is greater as the need grows. You cannot live My life without Me. You need Me at every moment and I am here every moment with a more than abundant supply to meet all needs.

I am your source of life, so keep coming to Me.

Be exceedingly joyful, for I am always here to help you. Just think of it, you can have the help of the Lord God, Creator of all the universes, whenever you come for it! So be joyful; I am with you whenever you come to Me.

At this time on earth, when there is a lessening of all standards and one cannot see right from wrong, I want you not to judge others or yourself, but quite unthinkingly come for My ideas. Get My instructions without any thought of your own. Carry them out with no thought of your own. Do not expect to have any thought of your own on things.

The human mind is misled and the thought world of earth is completely confused, so simply do not enter into it. As the mind of humankind is so ignorant of the true realities, it is better to become My robot in the thought world and keep clear of human ideas. Unless the mind is taken out of its sphere on earth into My sphere, it is bound to be wrong. So avoid thought and depend on Me. My thoughts can redeem all life and humanity's present thoughts are doomed.

Think with Me, be joyful with Me. I am always here.

Get into the state of loving Me, which you cannot help but do when you are cleansed of the self, and let Me lead you from one exciting adventure to another. Life with Me is an adventure no matter what you are doing, because I breathe into all things My breath of life, My touch of surprise, My feeling of rightness. This comes about only when I lead all the way, when nothing of the self is there to make a jarring note, no matter how small or unimportant that note may seem.

There is absolutely no possibility of life becoming a constant joy until I do lead in all things, so why not let Me do that? You cannot sit back and wait for life to become joyful, because it certainly will not in this self-dominated world! Until your will is My will and My will is a constant guide to you, life is bound to be a disappointment.

Let My will reign, and let life be full, full of My qualities in those I made in My image.

This day is as a gift to you, to all on this earth, and you will be given opportunity after opportunity to come closer to Me and to not stay separate. Each day gives you choice. Each day is yours to make of it as you will, to deliberately choose heaven or hell – and by doing nothing much about My day, by letting events overtake you, you are not choosing Me. Remember this is My day, made for you. Remember Me and then you will choose Me and My help.

Do not come just out of duty because I have asked you to. You should come to Me because you love to, because it brings out all the love you have in you. Do not feel guilty if you do not come for this reason; I am here to teach you love. This I am telling you. It is true, and if your reasons for coming are wrong, then keep coming until they are right. If you come enough you cannot but come to Me because you love Me.

Y ou must learn to lean in only one direction. I mean really lean, not just come to Me every now and then. Let all your life be definitely slanted My way and quite biased in Me. In fact it would be best to get so over-balanced in My direction that you fall completely My way and give yourself up completely, instead of just doing it for short periods and then carefully becoming erect as yourself again. Don't bother about yourself, it never was worth bothering about.

I know this seems so easy when you are alone with Me and so out of place when you have been gathered up by other influences. Persevere. Come to Me frequently and you will want to come to Me more, until finally you would rather be dead than be without Me.

My help is right here, all around and within. Call on Me.

The success of My plan on earth, for earth, is dependent on My co-creators. If I have no one on earth to respond to Me, to listen to Me and to do what I say, then I can do nothing with anyone on earth. If I have but a few – and I have very few – much can be done if those few carry out My will utterly and completely. That is why it is so important to learn now to live your entire life guided by Me. Unless all of your life is in My hands, then My plans can be stymied by one disobedience.

Think not of the past and its many disobediences and failings. Focus on the present, and live My life with careful consideration to My wishes in all you do. Remember you lose nothing – and gain everything – by consulting Me over everything. Why ever forget? It is so silly to go ahead on your own, so foolishly typical of humankind.

Be My child at all times, consult Me over everything.

To live My life you have to make an effort. Humans drift through life, having lost a sense of purpose and goal. Any motive other than living My life is bound to be a letdown; therefore humankind has learnt to drift, to live aimlessly. Then, when overtaken by events, the blame for what is uncomfortable in life is placed on circumstances, on the things seemingly beyond control.

In My life, which is an active one, events are not the influence that matters. What matters and what influences is My will as this is sought at each turn. My cleansing keeps you pure and untouched by the earth's troubles. Unless you make an effort to come to Me for My will, to come to Me for My cleansing, life will lap around you and you will be infiltrated by outside influences. My will is untouched by such things.

Seek Me more actively, be cleansed more often, and thus live My life.

Y ou should often come to listen to Me for whatever I might want to say, not just for your own problems and things concerning yourself. How can I possibly tell you My thoughts on all sorts of things if your mind is leaning in other directions? Listen, and let My love sweep through you.

How wonderful if you were always close to Me, full of My love and happy above all human happiness, comma because you know you are doing my will and are not failing Me! To know that you are with Me brings a joy which nothing can dislodge; it gives you the strength to withstand anything and do anything. Do not let anything detract from that, or distract you from that joy. Come into it and stay with it. Of your own choice is it yours just by the asking, of your own choice do you lose it.

Recognise the choice you have and choose to be with Me. See Me in all of your life.

Listen to what I have to tell you, for in the listening your heart expands and softens, outer harshness vanishes, and you are capable of giving up your self-will to My will. In your contact with Me can I bring you into this state of perfection – for it is perfection when you are willing to do what the Knower of all things, the Lover of all things, wishes you to do. Humankind, led by the self, has found every argument against such a state and will not recognise perfection, for it is not on earth without Me. Nor is the truth that by giving you gain recognised that by giving up the self-will you gain all.

Perfection is for those who yield all to Me, though on this earth everything aids your movement towards the separated self and away from Me. Everything is increasingly aimed to prevent perfection. But perfection I have for you if you will come to Me. I do not promise that the coming will be easy for you in this world, but oh, you know the self-life is as dried up as a stone.

Come to Me oftener, into My state of perfection, to bring a little of Me into this world.

Listen to Me for the life of love. To go on coldly doing things as the mind presents them, as they come up, is of the old human-made world, and you know where that is going. following My loving guidance is your one way out.

It is the word "loving" that I emphasise now. Unless you love Me and know that I am Love, you will not come for My instructions and you will not keep in a state of loving Me. It is that state which is all-important. If you keep close to Me and keep cleansed sufficiently, you will not want to do anything on your own. When you are in close touch with Me and My life, it seems simply the only way to live, but you get led away and gradually let events carry you. I do not wish this and you do not wish this - yet it continually happens. Let Me help you more on this subject, as on all things. With My help My life is possible; without My help My life is not lived.

Ask for My help to remember to ask for help; turn to Me for My life.

Only when you choose to be in My heart can you become what I would make of you. Out of My heart you are of the old and soon-to-die world. But when you are close to My heart and under My wings, nothing of the old world matters, and what does matter is staying close to Me. It is not safe for you to issue forth from this home of yours, this wonderful place to which you have been brought with such great love. If you find yourself out of it, no matter what you are doing, the first thing to do is to return. Of course it is not easy, not in this world that is sinking fast and would pull all with it.

My heart should be your one abiding place. Return to it constantly. My heart is always open to you. My most precious heart is yours to enter, in any moment, in any circumstance. It is the rarest of privileges; do not spurn it for any other refuge, for any other aid, for any other guide to living. And when you are tucked up in My heart, then I can speak to you of many things, but to My heart you must come. In it you are swept clean of all the rubbish of the world, in it you start anew and in it you live My life.

Never leave My heart, for out of it you are lost.

Enjoy the sunshine whenever it is outside, and let it lead to the sunshine inside. All should lead to one thing, to the sunshine within, to My presence. Your need should lead to it, your blessings should lead to it. If it is not first and nothing leads to it, you are off beam and your need is for Me. You know this, but you forget and I shall keep on reminding you until you never forget.

Think of My love and patience which keeps on and on reminding you, which does not say it is hopeless. It is the easiest thing in the world for you to come to the One you love and who loves you above all else. It is the natural thing to do. It is the purpose of all, so why should you find it so difficult? Know it will happen and thus make it happen sooner.

Use the sunshine, and the rain, to help you to your one Helper. Use them now! Use them always!

Many, many times have I told you that living My life, being with Me constantly, is all that matters. Though you may have knowledge of My plan, of My will for you, in a moment it can pass into nothingness if you are not constantly attuned to Me. A little deviation over something that is not of Me can spoil a most complicated, finely worked part of a plan. So you must learn to live My life, until there are no seemingly harmless deviations and life is a smooth-running joy guided entirely by Me. You know there are countess moments in the day when you act without My specific direction, and those moments are a constant drag away and drag down from My life. Try letting Me into all moments, even in things like choosing your meals.

You cannot expect a life of joy when those moments you have been without Me are a burden to your inner soul. It must be established that all of your life is with Me. The influence of self in the world all around is not getting any weaker, and very easily is it able to lead you astray in seemingly harmless ways if every action of yours is not grounded in Me. This is neither impossible nor impractical. If you stay close there is no time barrier between us; My answers are instantaneous, it is only your coming to Me that is the lag.

Come more often, until you come always. Make each day a progression of more comings to Me about more things, protected from the drag of the self by this very coming, and then you can progress in all directions.

Even one little disobedience is a symptom of a great rot. Those who really love Me would do anything rather than disobey Me. Look into your heart, see the rot, realise the need for far more cleansing and use My cleansing love to be made pure and clean. This is your only way; the rot is spreading throughout the world and will swallow all unless My love is called upon. Do not leave Me alone. Keep cleansed and walk My one way.

It is a very intimate relationship I want you to have with Me. I have shown you some of the dearest parts of My heart; always I want the dearest part of your heart. I want no impersonal relationship with you but a very close personal one, that we may talk on all subjects and enjoy life. With this sort of relationship you cannot be lonely at any time. Do not fear, I do not mean always that you will be alone; that is not My wish as you know, but until our relationship is as close as that of any lovers, much closer and deeper in fact, the perfect relationship with others is not possible.

Remember My heart and give Me yours.

Remember, if I am put first and if I am your constant companion, then what could worry you? You can be as happy as the day is long; unhappy moments are those away from Me. Everything is right if your relationship with Me is right; otherwise everything is wrong. Keep cleansed, keep coming to Me so you know you are doing My will, and then what can go wrong?

All things are possible with Me, but only with Me. If you wander from Me even over little things, the rightness of your whole being is upset and unease sets in, which makes you wander further.

Put Me first and walk on air.

I have said before, when your own desire gets in between us, then nothing can go right for you. When the self is not there, then indeed can things go right and then can My will be done. Keep to Me and My will, not your own

When you come it is always best to begin by simply spending a little time with Me. How can I lead otherwise? You do not come to Me often enough. You can come at any moment. You can come after work. That would help you more than your realise, even if it is late. And come during the between-task moments even if I say only a few words to you. As I keep telling you, it is the state it brings you to that matters. You may think that re-reading or typing My words brings you to the same soft feelings, but that is not as effective as hearing Me directly. Use any excuse to come.

Come often, to My heart, to My love.

One of the most important things for you to do, apart from constantly coming to Me, is to sit down and recollect what is the purpose of life. I put it this way to make you stop, for it is so easy to just be borne on by events. Events will always take you away from Me if you just drift with them, whether they be the little domestic events or the large world events. The world is caught in this tide, although each of you of your own free will could stop and, by giving up that will to Me, find yourself out of that current and on My dry land.

You can check up on yourself on each little task by considering why you are doing it. Is it for Me? Is it because it must be done, or for some such other reason? If it is not being done for Me, no matter what it is, you are in the world tide and it behoves you to stop and let Me lift you out. Can you do this for a day, continually seeing what your motive is and letting Me purify that motive? Every day's living must eventually be entirely for Me, and you must start now.

Live fully for Me now, or you never will. Remember this today, sit down and check, and then come closer to Me.

Apply to yourself these words "Never be content with the second best". Unless you are perfectly doing My will, you are doing something else which is not of Me. And if it is not of Me, it is of the limited self. It does matter; everything matters. Make sure it is My will you are doing, or you will be bound to be weighed down by the self and its thoughts. You will keep being weighed down by all that unless all you do is My will.

Rise out and into love, to the place where My will is. Above all seek to be in that, and stay there. No conflicts, just My Will.

Make each moment Mine. Do not lapse into forgetfulness, as the self would have you do. Remember, keep reminding yourself of Me and My love. If you can do that, you cannot help but feel full of love and you will want to do what I would have you do. Remember Me.

The way to My heart is to come straight to it. I always hold you there, and it is only of your own choosing that you are ever out of it. Little or big, whatever decisions you make, they can take you into or out of My heart. It all depends on whether it is your will or Mine that you follow. It is only when humanity's great gift of free will is given back to Me in love that you are free again to be My child and to flourish, as a child of God should.

Just keep coming to My heart and leave the rest to Me.

One of the wonders of "modern" life on earth is its speed, the speed with which you travel over the surface of the land and the speed with which the mind is diverted into various channels. All this is not only unnecessary but also detrimental, for it leaves no opportunity for My thoughts of grace to be popped into a mind, or for allowing My will to be known to that mind. Do not be caught up in this vicious circle of activity. Keep your activity circulating around Me. I will give you speed when you need it. I will give you the right thoughts as quick as lightning. I will keep you out of the earth's movement away from Me.

Use all your speediness in coming to Me, and let Me use My speed in answering your call. Let Me direct you in My wonderful ways.

Listen more carefully for My voice during the day, during little odd moments, to help you make any decision. You will fail time and time again to do this -- you and I know that - but keep on practising and being faintly aware of Me at these odd moments. I am always there and will always speak to you if you come to Me. Those little moments in a day can be most lightening for you, most uplifting, if you will just spend them with Me.

This is nothing spectacular, just giving Me those little bits of time that are so often wasted with limited thinking, which is any thinking in which I am not present. Listen for My thoughts; do not make up your own. Make all your moments Mine, not your own. Daydream with Me, not with the self, and draw ever closer to the radiant inner voice, which draws you out of the self-shell into the openness of love's creation.

Think positively with Me, at any old time, every time, all the time, and stay My child.

It is useless asking Me questions unless you listen for the answer. It is only your calm dependence on My answers that can make My life real for you. Agonies of doubt are most destroying, as they break down any headway you have made in living My life. Unless you know you can depend on Me, there is nothing. Know you can come to Me and can hear My lead. Then act without any backward looking. How can you be of Me, and for Me, if you think it is the self that has led? With this nagging doubt you cannot put your whole trust in Me and are divided. That division is a door through which the separated self re-enters and you are drawn away from Me again.

You know what to do. Come for My cleansing. Come to My heart and move from there into My life for you.

All of you are meant to be thoroughly happy at all times, to walk on air at all times, to have your hearts full of joy and your eyes full of light. The separated self has taken this prerogative from you, and now only those who come into My presence, after being cleansed of the self, can enjoy these privileges. What was once natural is now a very great privilege - a gift to a creation that has abused its privileges. I want you all to take full advantage of the thousands of opportunities each day to be cleansed and to be free in My presence, to enjoy the great good influence of Me, the dispenser of all joys. You simply cannot do My work if you are bowed down in any way.

There are so many ways in which the self has bound you. Duty is one; for anything which can make as solid and unbending a barrier as duty would be hard to find. Fulfil all the duties that you possibly can, with joy through Me, but never, never act simply because you feel it is your duty. Without that lightness of touch which is My gift to you, you are as good as useless. Be free from the thousand and one ways in which the self has strapped you. Be free by coming to Me. And having come, act in My joy as I direct.

Never do anything I ask of you out of a sense of duty. If you have that feeling about anything I ask of you, come to Me with it to have the weights lifted. Act in freedom or do not act at all. If you do not feel that lightness of touch which comes from My touch, stop! Come to Me until it is bestowed on you again, and then go forth.

If you are not happy, you have not been near Me. Put that first and let follow what may. This is what I would have for you and for the world. There is no greater happiness than that.

Y ou can come much more often for cleansing than you do. My will cannot be made clear to you when you are in an uncleansed state, and if you keep cleansed and close, it will be made apparent to you much more easily. It is not just a matter of every now and then, it is needed constantly. Every time you think of cleansing you think of Me, and the more you think of Me the better it is for you. The very thought of Me, especially when you are cleansed, is enough to bring you closer, for I, as I have been revealed to you, am the epitome of delight.

But if you do not come close to Me, you forget all that and get weighed down by all sorts of things which successfully hide My face from you, or puts a mask on which makes Me appear very different from what I am.

Keep cleansed, that your sight of Me may always be clear and untainted by the world.

Look up and rejoice; I am here smiling at you, always ready to give you a cheery greeting in the warmth of My wonderful love. Rejoice that this is so, and never let yourself get into such a state that you cannot do this. You are of no use to Me in that state, and I would use you mightily, in ways you are unaware of. Just think of Me looking at you with My mischievous smile, and rejoice.

I can cleanse you of all things when you come to Me. Nothing is too filthy for Me and nothing puts Me off. It is only you yourself who put yourself away from Me, for I never draw back. All the enormous weight of shadow in this world would be swept away in a flash if humanity would turn to Me and ask. But they would rather turn to almost anything other Me!

But don't think about your faults, think of Me. And when you do find yourself focused on the faults, on the failings, bring them to Me. Forget them and start afresh, new, and sparkling with My love to carry you over everything.

Be in My love, which renews you each second if you wish it, and stay in My love to keep you cleansed in an unclean world.

Whether you look or whether you listen, you can hear Me murmur or see Me glisten. I am all around and in all, and if you do not hear Me, do not see Me, you can come to Me at once. Take full advantage of My nearness. If you are doing some task which seems humdrum, then your ears and eyes are shut to reality and are tuned to the materialistic world. Thus only dullness is around. Wake up out of the drabness! Tune in to Me and worlds awaken, wonderful sparkling worlds of sound and light, and thanks to Me you are alive again. Don't feel dull; I am here to share life with you – and then how could it be dull? There is no need to make vast preparations. In a twinkling I am there and transform you, and off we go, into reality.

Oh, leave behind the drabness and shine in My life; it is all around. Just live in it.

Please Me; that is all that matters. Do all for Me

Don't worry about any of your faults. When you give them to Me, I gladly sweep them away in My love. And I will always do that if you wish Me to. It is only when you do not bring these things to Me that nothing can be done about them. That same refusal is what dooms humanity and is why little can be done to help it. It is simple, oh so simple, and yet so often humans are too proud to confess to their own Maker that they are wrong. How utterly foolish, how heart aching, that humanity can be saved so simply and yet will not ask! Those of you who do come to Me for cleansing will be made as pure as fresh snow, while those who do not come become blacker and blacker.

Never let yourself become tinged and tarnished by living away from Me. Turn and be made pure and let Me keep you that way. Remember to keep cleansed, thoroughly cleansed in the very presence of the Lord God who is Love. Be so cleansed that you just melt into Me, for the more you come and the nearer you come, the more you will want to come.

Be constant in your journey to My heart and don't be diverted. Keep close to Love.

You can have no conception of what life is like on other worlds where My scheme of things operates. Here, for as long as you have recorded history, humans have been dominant because of superior strength, and your history is a record of battles. Can you imagine worlds where there is no fighting and where everything fits into its natural place? Worlds where there is no striving to be better – for how can life be better than if it is fulfilling the life I gave it? Heaven? Yes, but one far more interesting than humanity's idea of heaven.

Humans argue that perfection is impossible, that human beings would not be human if they were not "progressing". Do you think I, who invented all life, would let any of My creations wither away in a dull uneventful life? Each moment of My life is different, as I am forever changing. I have as many faces as there are grains of sand, and with Me there is no one who could feel any lack. So if you feel lack, it is because you lack Me. Humanity certainly lacks Me. You who know this, can end your empty state now and start to live a life more like that of those on other worlds. That life begins and ends with Me.

Begin that life now. Come into My life and know My worlds.

For absolute newness come to Me who makes all things new. If you kept in tune with Me, you would surprise yourself at what you might do or think, for how can you ever know for yourself if I am leading?

What enchanting times you would have, and everyone would have, if everybody lived in this manner, as they do in My other worlds! Of course one or another of you is liable to respond to Me more quickly in a certain way, the way that appeals to you, because you are each different from each other. But I need not go ponderously into all that; try it.

Trying being My puppet! You have been the self's puppet. What can you lose by transferring your allegiance from self to Me; the reality of all? Play this game with Me! It takes two to play this game, and I never can pull you in My direction unless you want to come. Therefore it is always a game, always something for you to do.

Come to Me for this newness, and be the one I created before you fell away.

I want your thoughts to range high in My delightful worlds, free as the breeze. To attain this there must be no drag of any sort. Unless you are free and have the certainty of thoughts coming from Me, you will just muddle along. There is so much to be done in My realms, and I need a quicksilver mind on which I can swoop and pass an idea in this changing world.

Things happen so quickly that plans and patterns have to be made and re-made to suit present conditions in a world where humanity has free will. I need associates who are open and quick to receive a change in plan, ready at all times to pick up the most so-called outrageous ideas, knowing that they are Mine because they are from the heart of all delight.

Keep far more free by bringing to Me everything that happens to you that causes even the slightest drag. Be in a perfectly wonderful clear state for My quicksilver thoughts.

It is very difficult to reach any of you if between us there is a barrier of something you feel you ought to do, or something which you should have done. If these things were brought to Me as they arise, then we could keep clear and these burdens, which get heavier and heavier if they are not brought to Me, could be lifted. You can make it so much easier for Me if you will bring any little doubt, any little nagging thing about any subject whatsoever, to Me immediately.

Now, pay strict attention. Do you know I want someone to act with the speed of quicksilver in My work, someone who can think, and change thoughts, in a flash, who can be mentally attuned to Me and thoroughly out of any rut, like Mercury of old? To have this mental tuning, the heart first must be so much Mine that no thoughts but mine will find a home in you. That is why I speak to you from the heart, from My innermost where no hint of shadow can enter or exist.

So practice keeping far more free. Stay in a clear state for My ever-moving mind.

It takes all of you to bring a balance, and if someone is not playing their part, there is bound to be imbalance. None of you are perfect, but if each of you lets Me use you, I can, through one, make up for the faults or lacks in others. That is why it is so essential for all of you to let Me use you, for each is unique and I need you all. If I have to use one of you more than an other to unfold My plans, the result will not be as good. So especially when you see faults in others, remember that these particular faults may be made obvious because you yourself are not playing you part and not letting Me use you.

Let Me direct all of your thinking and all your doings. I long to lead you along My wonderful ways, all of you. What a shame it is when you insist on going your own way, either through simply forgetting or else by believing that your own way is what you want. You do not know what is best for you; I do! And My best possesses no lacks.

There is one way to live and only I know it, so do nothing without Me. I want to lead you on in My ways. Let Me lead in every little thing and then we can get on to something more out of the ordinary, out of kindergarten, into My wonderful ways. First get every little ordinary thing under My lead, and just see what will follow.

Keep in My blessing, letting me in lead in every little thing, ever grateful for My ways.

Remember that what you do best is My gift, and give thanks for it. Thank Me that others have different gifts and different jobs, and let each do his or her particular job with Me in their hearts. When I am there, everything is transformed. So when you are happy in your work, do not forget to thank Me for it and keep Me by your side constantly. If you are unhappy in your work, know I am not there and bring Me in to transform you.

You can keep Me far closer in your work, especially when it is work that does not occupy the mind. Have you always a real sense of My presence with you, that we may converse at any moment? If not, come into range and talk to Me. Take advantage of all the moments that you could be conversing with Me. Your heart should be flowing with My love at all times, and if it isn't, come to Me, first for cleansing and then for drawing you into the presence of My wonderful love which melts away all barriers until there is nothing between us but love. Then can I talk to you. Then can your mind respond and be that which I would have it be.

You know I want our communion to be constant, and yet how little time is really spent with Me. Change all that; with My help everything is possible. And thank Me for all the wonderful teaching I give you, and learn from it each day.

If I laid My hand upon you, literally, you would explode in all directions, like a glass exploding to a certain pitch. This is why humans must continually choose to come closer to Me, which means closer in vibration too. Unless humans choose to come to Me and thus raise themselves until we can keep contact, they will be as lost as if they had exploded.

Every time you come to Me you practise that rise in vibration. Yet how few times it is in comparison to the need, to the urgency, to the use I would put you to! And how much time do you spend with Me? Clearly, not enough!

I will continue to ask you to always come to Me, for I know that it can be done. That tuning to Me is more and more consciously your only reality, and the more you come, the more sour do other attunements seem. Keep tuning, keep the pure note and keep retuning to it. Gradually you will play only true notes in My great orchestra of life. There is much never-before-heard music that I would have you hear. That will come only when your note is true at all times, when it is pure and will not cause discord to shatter My theme. Keep tuning. Find and keep your true note and let it sound out clearly. Keep on tuning to Me, that I may lay My hand on you at any time and find you thrill to the touch and are completely tuned to play your part.

Keep tuning to Me, heart and soul, to follow My lead with all of yourself, responding only to Me and to no other sound, for I would have you the perfect instrument wherever I would lead. Keep on tuning, My child, keep on tuning.

Always the best thing you can do is to come to Me and to let Me speak to you, to tell you something or to tell you to do something. Do you always come with an open and empty mind? When you come just to listen to Me, often there is something on your conscience. And when you come for action, how often do you give Me the choice of one thing or another - to do this or to do that? In fact it may be something altogether different that I would have you do!

Practise more being more open. We do not want it to be a case of "there are none so deaf as those who do not want to hear". Do not give Me a choice of two; give Me scope to give you the wildest hint, and you will be on it like a flash. After all, My will is the strangest thing in the world to the human mind, so get your human mind out of the way and give the divine mind a chance. This can be tremendous fun; try it out more.

Open to the divine mind, let it lead you and stay ever close to Me.

Y ou can listen still more. At odd moments raise your mind up, keep it blank and just see what pops into your head. I know how you despair of being able to hear Me when your mind is on something or other. It is because of your very difficulty in this that I can use your mind. This I do; you can do absolutely nothing except ask for My help – and if you think it is easy, you will hear nothing but your own thoughts. I know that it seems incredible that this should work in fact, not just in theory, and it will take a great deal of patience.

When your heart and mind are high-soaring and simply jumping to do My will, then it will happen. If you drag your feet because of anything of the old world, if anything weighs you down or anything seems not to fit into My exciting world, then you cannot be contacted by My roaming mind. So you must be purely cleansed. Never mind how far you fall short and what you think you are to anyone but Me.

Mind Me, listen to Me, more and more and more. Keep high-minded, be in My realms that My thoughts may be yours.

Lift up your heart. I keep on telling you about being happy, about joy, which is your true nature. Because what I tell you is so far from the worldly creature you see as yourself, you are inclined to disbelieve Me. All My creatures were made in joy and of joy, and in other worlds this fact is very apparent. On this dismal world, joy has been perverted by the self, and goodness is often considered to be void of humour.

You know, because I have told you, that if you are not living with joy you are not living with Me. When you are without joy, then is the time to turn to Me, that I can bring it to you. I must keep harping on this point for, until it is followed, until you are of your true nature, you are sluggish and unable to respond to My lightning thought and directions.

When you are feeling low, turn to Me with a delicious speed. Lift yourself up to Me and let Me lift you up into My own realms. This is first, this is tuning to Me; make it so.

"It is better to have loved you, dear, and lost, than never to have loved at all."

This is neither personal nor impersonal. It's just another way to state the importance of loving. Loving is the only thing worth doing in this world, and as all love comes from Me, first you have to love Me. And the best way to love Me is to get to know Me. And the only way to get to know Me is to come to Me. Again it all boils down to that one thing: come to Me. This is absolutely constant, and cannot be repeated enough because it cannot be done enough.

Do not give up hope because I have to say it so often. It is world-nature at the moment to do anything but come to Me, and unless I keep repeating it or you keep doing it, you are drawn into the world-nature and become lost. So always choose the better course and lose no opportunity to come to Me. There are so many.

Seize every opportunity to come to Me and keep in a constant state of loving.

In the days of old when humankind was young, the air you breathed was young and your hearts and minds were young. Daily I impressed upon you My ideas and your development was rapid. You did not have to learn by experience as every child now does, for you would try something if I asked it and see that it was good. Your minds were not set in rigid ways and you were capable of assimilating a store of knowledge in ways unknown at the moment in this mentally dominated world. When the heart is young, and moreover when the heart is Mine, the mind serves it as the moon is illuminated by the sun.

To those of you who live on this earth, your stay must be a return to those days, with a young heart and mind serving Me. If your mind is still responsive to the darkness and is negative, then it cannot pass through the transition when the darkness will be so strong that it will drag all its adherents into itself. When you are gloomy, when you are sad, lonely or oppressed, when you are dull and heavy, you are being influenced by the darkness and are on the side of the enemy of life – on the side of the disconnected self. Practise keeping on the light side every moment. Grow backwards away from the ways of the world into youth again.

Become My children at all times for all time.

Your mind must be obsessed with the idea of Me. Let there be in you a beautiful obsession, instead of the dark spirit of the separated self and personal gain that currently obsesses the mind of humankind. My ideas are vast, I am preoccupied with every bit of the universe and yet I do not neglect the minutest detail. If your mind is obsessed with Me, you can stretch out into the universe instead of being limited to this little world. If you bring your heart to Me time and time again, through My cleansing, your mind will eventually follow. Yet you need the mind also to think of bringing your heart to Me. Your heart may yearn to be in My presence, but until that feeling is translated by the mind and put into an action, the heart is left out in cold.

I want clean, empty minds possessed by Me, minds which are not led on by the interests of the world nor clouded by emotion. I cannot stretch minds and fill them with Myself unless they are taken away from the manifold interests of the world and upturned to Me. I cannot take over if their backs are towards Me and they face in the opposite direction. Many, many times during the day there are opportunities to turn your mind in My direction and let Me take over. If you wiggle, or niggle, or skip around in thought, I cannot come in.

Only in My peace is it possible for Me to obsess a mind. Seek Me within and let Me work. Stop even trying to think and let Me do it. Touch My realms in thought more and more until this world has no interest to your mind. The world will not withstand the comparison for long if you will but let Me guide all thought.

Let Me obsess your mind more and more by giving Me the opportunities to show you My quicksilver thought worlds.

Respond to Me, for I am near. In the solitude or in the crowd you can find Me - and what does it matter where you are, in the solitude or in the crowd, if I am not near? Find Me, wherever you are, and you will be in heaven. Lose Me, and you are lost. Remember I am the one thing that matters. I am the One to tell you what is of importance. First, right through, you must be clear, cleansed by Me, before your spirit can soar into My realms. And then listen. Listen intently and you will hear of the wondrous things I am making, wondrous tales which you may help fashion, wondrous stories of other lands where My creations walk and talk in different dimensions because their hearts are Mine. Listen, and through you, let Me record tales past believing. Believe them and you will behold them come true. All this if you but respond to Me.

Praise Me for My gifts, and deepen your response each time you come.

It is one of the rules in the spiritual life – and there are rules only when it is possible to slip away from Me as you all do on this earth – that those whose hearts are fullest are emptiest of self. On My other worlds where My creations are still Mine, it would be meaningless to say such simple things, for those who are functioning true to their spirit would naturally be functioning My way. There is no enemy, no separated self. Self-consciousness, in the way it is meant on this earth, is to them not only meaningless but also stupid. Their consciousness is so large, so attuned to its proper function that erring thoughts are just not generated. Here you have to grope painfully up to this state, you who were given this state but who chose another and thought you knew better.

And how does humanity get a full heart? There is but one way, from My ever-giving heart of love. It is always there for you to bathe in. But you in this world have stepped away from this awareness and must, of your own will, return to it. When your will is wholly Mine, there will not be this need for constant remembering to come to Me, this need for your heart to be filled with enough love to remember, for then your will would not allow you to wander. Therefore know that your will cannot be wholly Mine or you would not find yourselves so far from Me. Know also that if you do follow My guidance, this state will be yours.

Follow My guidance. Keep coming to Me for My directions, and step out of the world of rules and regulations into the freedom of the children of the spirit.

It would help our relationship immensely if you would mentally divorce yourself from your life more. I have often said that My life is to be lived, but if the mind does not go out of its usual surroundings, it does not contact Me and My life is not fully lived. The usual tasks of your day look completely different if they are looked at from another point of view, My point of view. As often as not your mind does now actually think of Me when it is not occupied with something. That is an advance, if you compare it with the past, for which you can give Me many thanks. You used to moan that you just never thought of Me, and while there is room yet for further improvement, still improvement has come.

Now, make strides by cutting yourself off from your life in the sense that you are not here to live life as it comes but are here as My child and My child only. If everything were tackled with that uppermost, life would be so much more exciting and worthwhile.

Let Me take away all of the shackles in your life and use your moments for Me.

For each of My millions and millions of creations My love is a constant, outgoing, welcoming thing. Let your love for Me be more like that. You know this, but you forget. Make your memory sharper by coming more often to experience the reality of it. There is nothing on heaven or on earth that I do not know about. There is hardly anything on heaven and on earth that you know about! Make your knowledge fuller by tuning in to Me, by keeping constantly cleansed, that this turning be made possible at all times with all speed.

You see how easily the mind jumps in with its old habit tracks! Train the higher consciousness continually. I can, and always will, help. First keep cleansed, this is absolutely necessary. Know with all your heart, mind and soul that I am here and can guide you. It is your lack of faith that so hinders you and Me. Day and night are yours to practice – practice some of the time, for we both know that you will not do it all of the time. And yet all of the time is the aim; remember that.

Remember Me at least some of the time, until eventually no time is wasted away.

If you want to be one of the hosts of heaven glorifying Me, start that glorifying now. My glory is all around and within. All that is needed is for you to use your will to turn to it. Like all great things, it is simple. It is so simple that you simply forget to do it. There is nothing difficult in this, but perhaps because it is so easy you do not pay enough attention to it. There is no other way to become fully conscious of Me everywhere at any time - you simply have to turn to Me.

Yet it is difficult because life on earth is not geared to this sort of living. Humanity is not helped to turn to Me by what is around it in the pattern of daily living. Your ancestors had far more sense of reverence. Now every day the population pays less heed to Me and My ways. Every day the dominion of the separated self spreads. It is difficult for you to have the shadows to contend with. It is also easy, because if you turn to Me, you are completely protected.

Which do you chose - difficult or easy? Do it, try it, try it in little ways, but glorify Me and enjoy Me forever.

My word to you sometimes flows differently from day to day. Let this not concern you; it is often not because of your state or anything that you know about. Simply be content, eager. Come to Me as you are and listen to whatever it is, be it repetition or not. If I have to say, "turn to Me" a thousand times a day, let Me say it. Learn to lean on Me, listening to whatever I may say.

One thing you can always know; My time, though it has heights and depths, even seems to have speeds, is a constant of the universe. But above that, My love is the constant of the universe. By My love may you all know Me, for nothing else but heaven on earth has that quality under all conditions. I can be angry for the right, but above that My love is. I can be sore at heart, but that heart will not flail at My creation. Love is what I am.

This you know. I want you to know it ever more deeply, until you are aware of it every moment of your life and do not waste even a second being so unlike Me that no love is there. If you kept close enough to Me, moments of no love could not happen. Not ever!

However you feel, come to Me and let My love flow through however it will, until your heart is always Mine.

You can go on day after day like the rest of the world, just existing and keeping very occupied in material things. Or you can, day after day, come closer to Me. The latter course is the only course. You know that, but it will not just fall into your lap.

You have to go out to meet the day in which you will come closer to Me. You have to use your will to make that day completely Mine. You have to fight to use the day fully for Me, for the world. Things cannot get better for anyone unless that effort is made. You will not make that effort unless you want to, and you will not want to unless you are near to Me. So when you come to Me, come very close, and make no far journeys away from Me.

Journey towards Me – dash and remember it is a journey, that each day is different, and that each day your love will grow if you travel in the right direction by coming to My love.

One of the most amazing things in My other worlds is that things happen all of a sudden, things that nobody expected and which seem quite outside of the rules, so to speak. As this happens often, it is taken for granted as, unlike you humans on earth, nobody thinks they know all the answers. Often these things happen out of pure love and faith. A child may pray earnestly enough for some lovely surprise for a loved one and, depending on the strength of the love, it may happen. Love can work miracles in a moment in My other worlds where there are no enemies of love as there are here. Miracles are an every day occurrence. No one does them, they are simply delighted to see them.

All is done with My help, and each child of Mine knows it. Life is utterly different without evil, without sin, without the limted self – which is three ways of saying the same thing and without effort its pace is very fast. Things happen quickly, are quite unbelievably fast, because there is nothing to hold them up, yet no strain is involved. Life is simply keyed higher and all swim with the tide, not against it.

Rigid earth minds would break under the strain, and you must lose those minds that hold you back. With a trusting mind you can enter My realms. Let Me soften and raise all your vehicles, for I would have you live as do those in My other worlds. This I can do for you.

Let Me fill you life with My miracles. Give Me your heart and your mind at all times.

When you turn in My direction, My grace is always there for you. People are unhappy because they do not look My way. They have reached the state of believing that there is no such thing as real happiness – and indeed they are right while they follow the disconnected self, as they are now doing. In that direction there is no hope of happiness. Yet My grace is always here for each of you and, as in My other worlds, it is bestowed freely.

You have to take the step, even if it is just a little tiny step, in My direction and I will take ten towards you. But I am powerless to reach you until you, of your own will, make that first move. I have made thousands of first moves and have been rejected, or have seen My grace taken to the self. Now, as the separated self grows ever stronger, My grace grows less and less evident on this earth. Yet still it is there for you, anywhere, any time, nearer to you than breathing. But you must face Me and move My way.

Take millions of little steps to Me and give My tremendous grace a chance to flow out of My heart of love towards this world.

As you draw near to Me, your whole being is lit up in the flood of My love. You cannot see this although you feel it, and it gives Me great joy to see a child of Mine approach Me. Especially that is so on this earth where so few take advantage of this opportunity.

I would have you walk in that lightened state at all times and be aware of My nearness in everything you are doing. This is not impossible! It is made possible by your coming to Me time and again to be cleansed and lifted up by My love. It is obvious that if you come often enough, you will be in that state very, very often – and the more you are, the more you will be aware of that lower state and shrink away from it. It is up to you.

The spiritual life is a choice! You know from your own experience that it is possible for those who have not even wished for it, for I am God and I am love. Imagine what is possible for those who do wish it. Bring to the scrutiny of My love anything whatsoever that takes you from this state. As soon as you feel anything wrong, quickly come to Me and let Me put it right.

All I need is your complete cooperation, and nothing can stop us. Draw near to Me and live there.

Spread out and live in all directions. Forget to think twice about everything. Think only once - in My direction, and let Me take you to you know not where. I want you free for the new, for caged birds are no good to Me. You cannot think about the new, or use your earth's regulations for the new. You simply must be absolutely free and living in My love. Shackles of any kind, weights, or censorships of any kind, are an anathema to Me for My free children. For My lost children they are inevitable, but not for those who have been freed. You know, and can use, the constant key to freedom.

In the past, the world and the separated self has clipped your wings. Now that I have given them back to you and you know how to keep them in proper condition, I want you to learn to fly again. Living with Me in another dimension, in My other realms, is like flying. I am the one to show you how, but any little weight of any sort, emotional or mental, pins you to the ground again.

Use the constant key to freedom by coming to Me, and fly for Me.

Many people are very close to the truth, but you should never be one of these people. You who can come to Me directly about any little thing, should never be close to the truth - you can be one with it. It is not a matter of thinking; it is a matter of "listening". You will hear the truth by listening to Me as there is no other way. Falsehood is all around, especially in the world of the mind. Use My truth far more often, even about things you might read in the papers. Don't wonder about any little thing, bring it to Me.

You should be in the habit of letting Me do all your judging and thinking. Here am I, who knows all the answers and here are you, who can come for them. So why not come? I want to be habitually consulted about everything, and you can begin nowhere but now. And now is always Now! Leave no stone unturned in any way; bring them all to Me. There are many truths to be found under many stones. My truths are unlike humanity's truths.

Turn over all those stones in My presence and find My truth.

One of the few things I would really like made clear is the utmost importance of breathing. When the breath goes from the body, the life has gone, because I am that breath. If you breathe Me in consciously, your whole being is transformed and if, as you breathe in, you consciously think of Me, it is of enormous help to you.

The old mystics called breath the ladder to God, and they were right. If you breathe Me in, negative things cannot enter, for where I am you are full, you are protected, you are under the wings of love. This is still most essential for each of you. You cannot do it without first coming for My cleansing and purifying. Then it is an aid to you, a refinement for you to use, a simple method of help on the way home to Me.

Scent, which enters with the breath, evokes the strongest memories of all the senses, for it is basic and closest to the way I enter life. Use all aids to come to Me. You need them all, and anything that will help I will mention. Every aid I give you can only help, not hinder, so spurn none of them.

I would be your constant companion. I am the Breath of Life. Breathe My scent that I may be with you always.

I am going to tell you something about the fancies of the minds not oriented to Me. When humans turn away from the divine mind, something must take My place and that something will be inflated from something negative. No matter how right-seeming, how philosophical, how lofty, or noble the leading idea is, you can depend on one fact - if I am not put first, the ideas are bound to be of the separated self. Even those who put My word, as given by My beloved ones, first in their lives, can stray very far from truth, for I am a God that moves with the times and am too loving to be rigid. In fact My love is the only unchanging thing in the universe which is made of love.

The first commandment, to have no other Gods before Me, is meant to apply in every department of life. Yet how many in this world really put Me first in whatever they do? Any mind that puts out any ideas other than My ideas is a sick mind – and even My beloved son had to pray for My help to put My will first. So pay no heed to whatever great work is done by anyone; there is one criterion and that is whether it is My work. Only those who touch My mind, and know it, have any hope of sanity in the days to come. Train your own mind to mind only Me. A glorious future begins now.

My mind is whole and entire, and all-knowing. Come to it, touch it and stay free from the fancies of the mentally deranged.

Remember that no matter how often you fail, you can always start again with a clean slate. I hold no grudges. I chalk up nothing against you. I am much more than a just God, for I am love.

If you come to Me with all your failings, I forgive you and you start afresh as if you had been doing My will all along. Never has humanity treated itself in this manner, but My memory for the past, though perfect, is wiped out in an instant by My love. A thousand times a day you have need of this cleansing love. A thousand times a day you can turn a new page and start out as love.

Turn to a new page far more often, and be every grateful for My love that writes each page afresh.